The Edible
BALCONY

The Edible
BALCONY

GROWING FRESH PRODUCE IN THE HEART OF THE CITY

ALEX MITCHELL

PHOTOGRAPHY BY SARAH CUTTLE

KYLE CATHIE LTD

Published in Great Britain in 2010
by Kyle Cathie Limited
23 Howland Street
London, W1T 4AY
www.kylecathie.com

ISBN: 978-1-85626-938-4

10 9 8 7 6 5 4 3 2 1

Editor Judith Hannam
Designer Dale Walker
Copy Editor Helena Caldon
Prop Stylists Ali Allen and Cynthia Inions
Proofreader Ruth Baldwin
Index Alex Corrin
Production Nic Jones, Sheila Smith and Lisa Pinnell

A Cataloguing in Publication record for this title is available from the British Library.

Printed and bound by C & C Offset Printing Co., Ltd.

Contents

Introduction

It's the ultimate escape from the urban buzz. Imagine sitting high off the ground in a Mediterranean-style idyll surrounded by grapes, tomatoes, lemons, and salad so fresh that it squeaks while the traffic roars far below. From a few pots on the balcony to an entire orchard on a roof terrace, the possibilities for growing fruit and vegetables off the ground are endless – even if you live in the heart of the city. Not having a garden doesn't mean you can't be eating delicious, organic salad, herbs, vegetables and fruit every day of the year.

Urban buzz: beehives and crops co-exist happily on a London rooftop

From bijou balconies to sleek, decked roof terraces with a view of the city skyline, your own little bit of outdoor space in the city has always been something to covet, but now more than ever we're embracing the chance to green up our environment. In London alone, more than 60 per cent of new apartments now have outside space – three times the figure of ten years ago. These budding balcony gardens are not just growing flowers, either – after all, why just fill the space with geraniums when you can grow fruit, vegetables, herbs and salads and

benefit from delicious fresh organic food at your fingertips?

Balconies are ideal places for growing edible crops, as they are often very sunny and high out of reach of pests such as slugs and snails. Many crops grow happily in containers and a surprising number are beautiful too – from lush fig trees to silver thyme, yellow climbing beans and frilly lettuces. You can gather strawberries when they're properly ripe, not picked hard for transport on a lorry for several days. You can eat peas and carrots before their sugars have turned

your table – grow it on your balcony and you can reduce this to a few metres.

In cities all around the world, people are discovering how wonderful it is to grow fresh fruit and vegetables, and realising that you don't need an awful lot of space to do it. Urban residents, many of them young and with no experience of growing food, are tapping into the pleasure of eating their own produce straight from the plant and marvelling at how they can grow it right there outside their window.

Balconies may be small, but that inspires people to find creative ways to use every available bit of space. Whether you're after an exotic feel, a sophisticated herb garden, or simply want to cram in as many crops as you can in a jumble of tumbling fertility, a balcony is a theatre set waiting to be dressed. People are finding ingenious ways to grow delicious crops – from salad leaves in bottles to herbs in hanging shoe-organisers. Invention, individuality and expression are the key words for this new breed of urban farmers; rolling acres are not necessary – all you need is a few pots.

There are currently around 100,000 square metres of green roofs in London, a figure that the city plans to double by 2012. As for potential food-growing spaces, even tiny spaces add up. The National Trust estimates the UK has 600 acres of windowsill space capable of growing food crops. If you added all the flat roofs in London together you would have a space 24 times the size of Richmond Park. That's room for an awful lot of tomatoes. And why stop at fruit and vegetables? A beehive takes up less space than you'd think, so how about producing your own honey several storeys up?

Whether it's guavas in Mumbai, a quirky Manhattan fire escape of herbs and salads or olives ripening in the heart of London, *The Edible Balcony* mixes inspirational ideas with practical advice to show you how to create a beautiful, flourishing outdoor space however many floors up. From an easy edible balcony that can be set up over a weekend to individual styling tips using recycled and salvage materials, advice on producing exotic fruit you never knew you could grow and even on making a do-it-yourself salad wall, this book is full of ideas to turn your balcony or roof terrace into a sky garden packed with gourmet pleasures.

to starch, and tomatoes still warm from the sun. Grow things yourself and you can fill your space with unusual crops you can't easily buy in the shops – stripy tomatoes, beautiful flecked borlotti beans or tangy buckler's leaf sorrel.

Whether it's a few herbs that you're after or pot after pot of carrots and potatoes, a balcony is the ideal place to get growing. You may not be self-sufficient, but you'll enjoy delicious fresh food picked straight from the plant, and know exactly how and where it was grown. The average salad has travelled 1,400 miles to reach

Why should I grow food on my balcony?

Your balcony, however small, is a valuable splash of green in a concrete urban jungle, but its benefits are far more than just aesthetic: When you plant edible crops and flowers on your balcony you are not only creating a beautiful, relaxing haven and a handy source of ingredients for your lunch, but you're benefiting the wider environment, too.

It looks better

A bare balcony is a depressing sight and a wasted opportunity – often an arid lozenge of steel and glass. But fill it with plants and it becomes a vibrant place that softens the hard lines of the city and gives you a chance to pause and breathe.

It tastes better

Grow fruit and vegetables on your balcony and you can experience gloriously fresh food – sweet carrots, meltingly ripe strawberries and springy salad leaves. You can also grow things you can't easily buy, such as purple mange tout and yellow cherry tomatoes. With the merest effort you can be self-sufficient in herbs and never again have to let those plastic packs of parsley from the supermarket turn to slime at the back of the fridge.

It reduces food miles of fruit and veg

It's obvious really, but there is something undeniably satisfying about being able to pick a salad from outside your kitchen and know exactly where and how it was grown. When you start

Hospital grows tomatoes hydroponically on its roof – yielding 200kg of tomatoes annually and reducing the heat on the roof. In cold countries, planting on roofs has the opposite effect – it reduces heat loss from the roof, so cutting down on expensive heating costs.

It reduces pressure on city drains

Every time it rains in a city, water rushes into the drains where, in the case of London and New York, it mixes with sewage before being processed. This system worked well when it was constructed years ago, but since then an awful lot of roads, buildings, pavements and car parks have been built, meaning more rainwater is forced into the drains as opposed to being safely absorbed by the soil. This is why people get so vexed about front gardens being paved over for car parking. A sudden heavy downpour can overload a city's storm drainage system so that, unable to cope, it dumps the rainwater-sewage combo in rivers or the sea.

By planting on your balcony or roof you create a sponge that holds rainwater for some time before it runs down into the drains. Even a small delay of 20 minutes can make the difference between a functioning city drainage system and one that is dangerously overloaded, so by greening your roof or balcony you can make a really useful contribution. Capturing rainwater in water butts to use on your plants is an even more helpful step.

It reduces air and noise pollution

Plants on a roof or balcony will improve air quality by absorbing carbon dioxide emissions and releasing oxygen. A green roof will also absorb urban noise pollution – from aeroplanes to traffic.

growing some of your own food, you quickly learn about and appreciate what is in season and what is local. When you have eaten French beans you have grown yourself, those little cellophane-wrapped green sticks flown in from thousands of miles away don't seem so convenient after all.

It keeps cities cool

Built-up areas trap heat, making average ambient temperatures in cities up to 3 degrees warmer than in the countryside. With global warming set to continue, urban temperatures will only increase. Planting on roofs and, to some extent, balconies, insulates buildings from the heat of the sun by as much as 20 per cent, thus reducing the need for expensive and energy-devouring air conditioning. In Osaka, in Japan, sweet potatoes were hydroponically grown (that is, in nutrient solution rather than soil) on the roof of an office block and this cultivation method was found to protect the roof significantly from the heat of the sun, as well as provide a useful harvest. In Singapore, Changi

Planning your piece of edible sky: balcony basics

A garden high above the ground is a unique environment with its own advantages and challenges. The sun may shine all day and pests such as slugs and snails struggle to climb up to reach your delicious crops, but the wind might just take your hat off. Here's how to make sure your garden in the sky is safe, peaceful and productive.

Is it going to stay up?

Balconies are generally constructed to support the weight of people, so a few pots are usually not going to be a problem. If you're worried, though, use lightweight pots, such as plastic liners hidden by woven willow baskets, and site them nearer to the house or over load-bearing supports. Similarly, roof terraces will also have been designed to withstand large loads and should have no trouble holding up the number of potted plants you'd expect in an average domestic setting. However, if you're thinking of more ambitious projects, such as very large pots, raised beds or laying soil over the whole roof, it's a good idea to consult a surveyor or structural engineer first. Obviously, if you're planning to create an 'unofficial' roof terrace – customising a flat roof that wasn't built to have people and plants on it – you will need to seek the relevant planning permissions first as well as advice from a structural engineer to find out if the roof will need to be reinforced.

Load-bearing areas are generally positioned around the edge and above internal supporting walls, and it's here that you should put heavy pots, water features and seating. If you have a balcony that is suspended from the side of a building, don't put lots of heavy pots in one place; rather, spread the load around, putting the heaviest items nearest the building.

Earth, wind and sunshine

Sunny? Shady? Does your hat stay on? These are the sort of things you need to think about when you plan your garden in the sky. But there is one thing you can almost always be sure of: up high it is generally much more exposed than at ground level, so you will undoubtedly be contending with the wind.

There are two ways to deal with the wind. The first is to plant wind-tolerant plants; many of these are coastal – hedges of grasses and bamboo or those that form dense evergreen blocks, such as box or *Elaeagnus × ebbingei*. In the edible world, wind-tolerant crops may include hardy herbs such as rosemary and bay, low-growing crops like salads and strawberries, tough fruit trees like olives, or vegetables like carrots, potatoes or dwarf French beans.

The other solution is to construct some form of protection by erecting screens. Trellising or bamboo or reed screens, available from all garden centres, are great for this since they filter the wind a little, rather than forming a barrier that whips it up, over the top, then down again to scatter your Sunday papers. Trellising, of course, can be used to support climbing plants – adding valuable height to any garden design. Bamboo or reed screening is less appropriate for growing plants up, but it is gentle on the eye, extremely good value and can be easily fixed to posts using plastic cable ties. Bear in mind, though, that screens do tend to block out the

view, so you may have to compromise on height if you want to see that lovely urban skyline. Also, work out which direction the prevailing wind generally comes from before you put up any windbreaks, as you don't want to block out your views needlessly. This is as simple as standing on your balcony for a couple of minutes over a period of several days and judging which way the wind is blowing.

Wind will also have an effect on the pots you can use to plant your crops. The lighter the pot, obviously the less weight you'll be adding to your balcony or roof terrace, and the less difficult it will be to get it up there in the first place. However, the downside is that light pots can skitter across a roof terrace on a windy day – even furniture can travel the length of a roof if you don't choose wisely. If your balcony or roof terrace is windy, either secure light containers by tying them to railings or fixings or choose heavier ones such as terracotta that won't budge in a breeze. Low, heavy trough planters are the most wind-resistant of all.

One of the great benefits of sky-high spaces is the amount of sunshine you get. Anyone with a small urban garden will know how frustrating it is when your precious crops and flowers – not to mention your sunbathing zone – are shaded by other buildings and trees. Up high, this is much less likely to happen. Of course, the opposite can then occur: too much exposure to sun, scorched plants and a need for endless watering. But in a north European climate this isn't likely to be a huge problem, and it's easy to attach shade screens to the railings of a balcony or string up one of those shade sails if things get really Saharan. For a more permanent shade structure, you could attach a retractable fabric awning to the

Water butts are a
valuable addition
to any balcony

Water, water everywhere

All roofs – even flat ones – are generally built on a slight fall so that rainwater can drain away into gulleys or drains. Check which way the fall goes on your roof and bear it in mind when positioning pots, as water will seep out from pots when you've watered them and you won't want to block its escape by putting something in between them and the drain, such as a raised bed or planter.

All roofs have a waterproof membrane and it's really important that this is not pierced during the construction of your roof terrace, or else rainwater will then drip down and get into the building. Even installing lights on spikes could damage a membrane, as could securing pergola uprights or railings – so be aware.

The whole issue of saving rainwater has become an important one of late, and we are continually urged to reduce the amount of water that is lost into the drains. Collecting rainwater in a water butt from the roof is a great idea in a roof garden, because then you'll have it easily to hand to water your plants – something you'll really appreciate when the alternative is carting it in quantities from the kitchen several times a day, or the expensive fitting of an outside tap.

'I wouldn't lean on that if I were you'

Run a mile if you ever hear this while standing in a roof garden! It goes without saying that any balcony or roof terrace needs to have a secure barrier around it, but do ensure that any railings or banisters are firmly fixed before you start creating your edible sky garden. These railings may well end up covered with plants or windbreak screens, so you must make sure they can take the extra weight this will bring before you get happy with seeds. When putting planters or seating around the edge of a balcony garden, make sure they couldn't be used as a platform for children to climb up.

building that you can roll down on hot days and roll back up if the wind really picks up.

Don't write off the bits of your outside space that seem unpromising. Areas that are hidden around corners or are shady all day long could not only be useful for storage of pots, compost, the barbecue and deck chairs, but could also be the perfect place to put a wormery. This is an excellent way of turning all your uncooked kitchen scraps and plant prunings into a nutritious compost that you can then feed to your plants in a circle-of-life kind of way. When deciding on the position of dining tables and chairs, think about where the sun hits the balcony in the morning and at lunch and supper time. Is there potential for a glorious sundowner spot, for a couple of chairs and a cool drink after a hard day?

Making the most of your space: design basics

Wander through a tunnel of climbing beans. Tiptoe to a deckchair hideaway clothed in raspberries and bright orange squashes. Your balcony doesn't only have to be productive, it can also be a private paradise where you let your imagination run riot. From your choice of flooring to tomatoes and nasturtiums tumbling down from above, here's how to make your balcony look as good as it tastes.

What are you looking at?

You may be up high and therefore out of reach of cars, pedestrians and plant-munching slugs, but if you live in an apartment block, chances are you're not far away from other people. Before you reach for a screen or fence to give you privacy, though, consider using plants instead. A mop-headed bay tree in a pot, for example, could block out the curious eyes of any neighbours all year round; evergreen box or rosemary can make a dense low screen; tall bamboos and grasses are happy in containers and will filter the wind, too; while a grapevine clambering over a pergola will give you not only privacy but also lovely dappled shade. Other edible evergreens such as rosemary and sage can be useful as well, not to mention a smorgasbord of non-edible climbers and bushes.

If your space is big enough, you can also think about creating rooms within rooms with trellis screens forming different areas – perhaps for eating, sunbathing, or as a play zone for the kids. If your rooftop is long and thin, it's always a lovely idea to create separate 'rooms' with staggered screens so that you can't see to the end of the terrace, but are led on curiously to zigzag round each 'bend' to find out what comes next. From the point of view of edible plants, this also works really well since it provides lots of useful space for climbing plants such as beans, cucumbers, squashes and kiwis, as well as those that need tying in to vertical supports, such as trained fruit trees and cane fruit such as blackberries, raspberries, tayberries and cordon tomatoes. Separating out areas provides shelter from the winds and useful shade in very sunny gardens too.

Balconies as outdoor rooms

With a floor, three walls and often even a roof, balconies really have more in common with indoor rooms than they do traditional gardens. This can make them great fun to design, as well as much less intimidating to first-time gardeners who would baulk at the thought of planning an expanse of lawn and flower beds. If you think of your balcony as another room, it frees you up to dress it in your own style and experiment with colour and materials.

From the floor up

Many modern roof terraces and balconies are decked with wood, which is a stylish and relatively light and inexpensive choice. This material also evens out uneven surfaces and is great for hiding lighting cables or watering underneath. Make sure you buy your timber from a properly managed source, since many tropical hardwoods are non-sustainably harvested. Wooden decking is easy to cut for any shaped space and, for an aesthetic consideration, by laying the boards in different patterns you can play around with how the eye takes in the space. If you have a long, narrow

Evergreen edibles
such as bay
and rosemary
will give you
privacy all year

space, lay the boards across-ways to prevent the eye rushing down to the end, which makes the area feel narrower. Similarly, mixing up the direction of the boards in panels gives visual interest to an otherwise bland block.

When altering the flooring material of any balcony or roof terrace, you must always make sure that rainwater can run off freely. Standing water on any balcony or roof floor surface is not a good thing, as over time it can rot the waterproofing and then leak through into the building below. So this means that any decking should be laid on wooden joists to allow the water to run through the cracks in the decking and flow away down the guttering as normal. When laying the joists, makes sure that they do not block water flow either.

If decking seems too much trouble and you want something quirky with a sense of humour, what about artificial turf? Simple to unroll and cut to shape, once it is laid all it needs is a quick sweep now and then.

Looking up

As well as cramming pots into every possible corner, don't forget that there's a lot of potential growing space up above too. Hanging baskets can grow a surprising amount of delicious food – from strawberries to salad and tomatoes. There have been exciting breakthroughs lately in edible walls, such as modular grids filled with rockwool into which crops are planted and then fed and watered hydroponically (see p. 146). You can cram all sorts of herb and salad crops into these walls and they fit snugly against the wall of a building.

For the less high-tech-minded, don't underestimate the value of simple staging – wooden benches around the edge of your balcony or terrace will double your growing area and make it look wonderfully lush, and it can also provide useful shade for less sun-worshipping plants, such as mint, chives, sorrel and parsley. Balcony railings themselves are perfect ready-made supports for climbing plants to twine up and to tie tomatoes and trained fruit trees to.

An archway or pergola is a wonderful thing to include, too, providing lovely dappled shade, a focal point and plenty of growing space for climbers such as grapes, kiwis, runner or French beans and squashes of all wonderful shapes and colours. If you have a small balcony, why not make a quirky pergola by running some wires up from the balcony railings to the building wall, as high up as you can, and grow crops overhead? If you have more space, think about putting up an arch – whether wooden or metal doesn't matter, as long as it can be secured so it doesn't blow over in the slightest wind.

Laying wooden
decking boards
diagonally makes
this tiny balcony
appear larger

What pot?

There are no rules when it comes to choosing what container you want to grow your plants in – from an eclectic jumble of differently sized pots in terracotta and plastic to sleek metal troughs hugging your balcony edge, the style of your sky garden is up to you. There are, however, a few considerations worth bearing in mind to get the best out of your plants.

Generally, the bigger the container, the lower-maintenance it will be, in particular when it comes to watering and feeding, which you won't need to do as often. Small pots and window boxes need watering every day in the height of summer, while large tubs can manage for three or more. Treat large pots as mini beds; mix trees, for example, with low flowers and crops such as lettuce, strawberries and herbs and you can fit a lot in. For flexibility, planters on wheels are a great idea as you can move them around to screen different areas, as well as to benefit from the best of the sun.

You can have wonderful planters made to fit the space exactly, but it's also easy to find cheap containers in garden and DIY shops; a galvanised dustbin can look just as stylish as bespoke troughs. A smart look can easily be achieved if you keep uniformity in mind. Mixing up too many materials can distract the eye and chop up the space visually – black plastic here, terracotta there – in a way that keeping everything wooden, for example, would not. A range of galvanised metal containers is an ideal choice: light to carry, modern yet mellow on the eye, and easily available in all shapes and sizes, from window boxes to enormous pots for fruit trees. Another good choice of container material is fibreglass, which is lightweight with a clean, modern look. Terracotta is a classic – handmade pots are far more attractive, yet more expensive, than factory-made versions – although they are not the lightest of containers. Troughs are ideal for balconies because they fit neatly around the edge, using the space well and thereby maximising the crops you can grow.

For instant gratification, flexible plastic tubs, available in any garden centre or DIY shop, are a good choice: cheap, light, large enough for any crop and so vividly coloured they'll cheer up anywhere. There are also plenty of lightweight planters specifically designed for growing fruit and vegetables, many made from thin plastic or woven material you can simply fold up at the end of the season. Either brightly coloured or sold with woven willow panels to prettify them, these are roomy enough to be really useful.

Any planter that has a built-in reservoir is ideal for roof or balcony gardeners, as it really cuts down on the watering needed. Large, hungry crops, such as tomatoes, aubergines, squashes and peppers, are particularly well suited to these types of planters, often known as 'self-watering containers'. Earthbox is a popular brand, but if you don't want to buy one, you can easily make your own self-watering container (see How You Make It Personal, p. 73).

Since wind is always a factor on balconies, wide-bottomed containers are best because they are less susceptible to blowing over. The classic container (tapering to the base) is not ideal, though anything can be kept upright if you tie it against supports. Troughs, however, are virtually wind-proof and are a great use of space as they can be lined up along the balcony, fitting in lots of crops and also forming a uniform border.

Mini raised-bed kits are also a good option if you're after a more traditional allotment look. Being wider, they spread the load, and if they're made of a lightweight material, the only significant weight comes from the soil. Be sure to position them so that any water that drains away is not blocked from reaching the guttering.

Go grow bags

Grow bags are fantastic for growing crops in, since they retain water really well and come with fertiliser already in the compost. They're light to carry up stairs and are so slim that they fit neatly against a wall – so even the narrowest balcony can manage a few and still leave space for a table and chairs.

Potatoes can also be grown in grow bags if you turn them vertically and cut the top off. Make a few drainage holes in the bottom of the bag and remove half the compost, putting it aside for later. Plant three early potatoes so the tops are about 15cm below the surface of the compost and roll down the sides of the bag to the new compost level. As the plants grow, keep adding compost to cover them, rolling up the bag as you go. Keep well watered. Harvest when the plants flower – about 12 weeks after planting.

BEST CROPS FOR GROW BAGS

* Tomatoes
* Sweet peppers
* Aubergines
* Cucumbers
* Chillies
* Lettuce
* Rocket
* Basil
* Radishes
* Runner and French beans
* Courgettes
* Squashes
* Peas
* Chard

Window-box winners

You can grow a surprising amount of food in a window box, as long as you choose the right plants. Try to make the container as big and as deep as possible, in order to widen the choice of what you can grow and to cut down on watering. Obviously, if you are up high do take care to secure any window boxes well – bracket kits can be picked up easily from garden suppliers – or consider balcony planters that are divided, so they 'straddle' balcony walls safely and need no additional fixings. If you are at all worried about them falling, place them on the inside of your railings.

BEST CROPS FOR A WINDOW BOX

* Herbs – basil, chives, coriander and parsley will all thrive in a medium-sized box, while rosemary, thyme, sage and oregano need a deeper, larger one
* Salad leaves
* Radishes
* Spring onions
* Dwarf French beans
* Bush or tumbling tomatoes (not cordon varieties)
* Strawberries
* Chard
* Edible flowers such as nasturtiums, violas and marigolds
* Chillies
* Pea tips (see p. 39)

BEST CROPS FOR HANGING BASKETS

* Tumbling tomatoes, such as 100s and 1000s or Tumbler – 1 plant per basket
* Strawberries – 3 plants per basket
* Salad – lettuce, rocket and others
* Runner beans – try sowing 3 or 4 seeds and watch them trail down the sides in a waterfall of flowers and beans
* Spring onions
* Pea tips (see p. 39)
* Herbs – coriander, chives, parsley, thyme, oregano, chervil, tarragon and basil

When growing crops in a hanging basket there are two things to think about. The first is that you don't have to buy one of those traditional basket kits from a garden centre – the ones with an iron frame lined with moss, coir, sisal or jute – or a woven rattan basket if you don't like the look of them. The pluses of these are that they're convenient, sturdy and come with their own bracket kit, so they are easy to install, and you can also be sure they can take the weight of any crop you put in them. However, some people find them generic and old-fashioned. So don't be afraid to customise your own hanging containers using strong twine or chains; you can hang any light container with holes punched into it for drainage and to attach the hanging ties. From colourful tins to kitchen colanders and large plastic containers, these can be much more quirky, stylish and individual than the made-to-measure numbers.

The second consideration with hanging baskets is that, being relatively small, they will dry out more quickly than larger pots and so they need frequent watering. You can mitigate against this to some extent by mixing in a handful of water-retaining gel with the compost before you sow or plant (this swells up with water when you soak the basket, gradually releasing it back into the compost over time), but you'll still need to water the baskets every day or two in hot weather.

Inspiration from above

Of course, when balcony gardening your potential growing space is not limited to the horizontal; one of the most exciting things about growing plants up high is how much you can exploit your wall space and any railings or barriers you have. Attach trellis panels to the wall to grow plants up, and if you have railings or a metal grid barrier, use them for peas, climbing French beans, runner beans or colourful, rampaging squashes.

New vertical gardening products are being launched all the time – such as the Polanter, a funky plastic tube you fit to the wall and into which you can plant salad, herbs, flowers or even tumbling tomatoes, peas and strawberries. Woolly Pockets, felt pockets made from 90-per-cent recycled bottles, are deep enough for aubergines and peppers; a whole wall of these pockets can look really stunning and hold a surprising amount of crops.

Hang in there

Hanging baskets not only bring life and colour into a balcony space, but they can also produce a surprising quantity of food. The hard lines of a balcony can be softened by a row of containers suspended either from the 'roof' (if another balcony juts out over yours), the wall of the building behind, or the balustrade along the front. Just as with window boxes, it's very important to make sure any baskets are well secured – a heavily laden hanging basket of tomatoes could do some serious damage falling onto the ground below. So, again, to allay your fears, hang baskets on the inside of the railings or where they would fall only onto your balcony floor.

Go up a level

Another good tip that immediately doubles your planting space is to fit staging around the edge of a balcony or roof space – low benches or boxes such as fruit crates are ideal. You can then grow shade-tolerant crops such as salads, parsley and mint on the floor level, with sun worshippers such as tomatoes, courgettes and French beans above. Ladder-style pot stands or racks mounted on the wall do the same job.

Compost and plant food

One of the beauties of balcony gardening is that you definitely won't need to buy a lawn mower. There are, however, a few essential bits of kit that are worth getting your hands on before you start turning your balcony into an edible Eden.

Which compost?

Obviously, when you first plant anything, you need to buy compost. The one you buy depends on what you are growing: annual vegetables, fruit and flowers are happy with one that is multipurpose, organic and peat-free;

acid-loving crops such as blueberries need ericaceous compost; while fruit trees and bushes, which will live for many years, will benefit from a soil-based compost such as John Innes No. 3, which releases its nutrients slowly. Unless it is stated otherwise in this book, assume that any crop is happy to be planted in multipurpose compost, and for any suggested planing, an organic peat-free compost should be used.

Won't I have to replace the compost constantly?

Luckily, no, or you would have a back-breaking time ahead of you, constantly carrying new bags of compost upstairs – also it would not be a very sustainable way of gardening, and pretty expensive.

Hungry crops, such as tomatoes, potatoes, sweet peppers, aubergines, courgettes and squashes, do need fresh, fertile compost to grow really well, but others, such as carrots, peas, beans, salad and herbs, don't require so many nutrients. If you grow hungry crops in fresh compost you can then reuse it for less hungry crops. To reuse compost, sift it through your fingers, removing as many roots as you can since these can stop water draining through and make it difficult for new roots to spread out. You can add the old roots to your wormery or compost bin. Top this old compost up with a third fresh multi-purpose compost and, if you have a wormery, a few scoops of fresh worm compost. A handful of slow-release plant food will revitalise old compost too.

Worms on the roof

Measuring only about 60cm square, wormeries are ideal for balconies and are fantastically helpful – not only can the worms digest kitchen waste, old roots and prunings from a past crop, but by adding a few scoops of highly nutritious worm compost to your old compost you can inject new life into it, thus making it ready for a new crop. Worms also produce a highly nutritious liquid feed for your plants. (See p. 114 for more information.)

Feeding and drainage

Apart from the plants, seeds, compost and containers, of course, there are a few other items that are worth buying to set up your balcony.

Most crop plants need feeding, and a good all-rounder is organic, sustainably sourced liquid seaweed feed that you dilute according to the instructions on the packet. (Any tomato feed can be used in the same way.) A bottle should be enough to see you through the whole growing season and will ensure your plants get all the nutrients they need.

Herbs and fruit trees will benefit from a few additional handfuls of horticultural sand or grit being mixed into the compost when they are first planted (which will improve drainage), so it's a good idea to buy a bag or two of these as well.

Add a garden trowel, a pair of secateurs, some garden twine and bamboo canes and you'll be ready to start creating your edible balcony.

The Easy Edible Balcony

Many of us dream of growing our own salads, herbs and tomatoes to eat at home, but worry that we can't spare the time and energy to do it properly. Visions of returning to brown, dry plants after a weekend away spring instantly to mind, or fruit and vegetables that never ripen. But if you choose the right crops and follow a few simple growing tips your edible balcony can flourish without making many demands on you at all, even if you are a total beginner. It doesn't take long to set it all up, either; over a weekend you could transform your balcony from a bare, grey space to an emerging wonderland of shoots and fruits.

Plants not seeds

If you don't have the time or the space to raise plants from seed, buy seedlings from garden centres or online suppliers and set up your entire edible balcony over a weekend. Plants ordered from catalogues or websites will arrive via the post and can simply be popped into the compost as soon as they appear. You may not be able to choose from quite the number of varieties available as from seed, but the range is expanding all the time.

Crocks away

When planting up containers it's traditional to add a layer of 'crocks'– pieces of broken terracotta pots – to the bottom to aid drainage. These are not always easy to come by, so you can use chunks of polysytrene packaging instead – the trays that seedlings come in from garden centres are ideal. This material has the added benefit of being really light, too, which is perfect for gardening on balconies.

Large containers need less frequent watering than smaller pots.

Easy peasy – tips for hassle-free balcony gardening

Big is best

When choosing containers, make life simple for yourself by not filling your balcony space with numerous tiny pots, as these will dry out the minute you turn your back. Instead, use large, lightweight containers, such as those made of plastic and galvanised metal. Troughs are ideal since they seem to hold their moisture better than round pots and fit snugly around the edge of a balcony, nicely positioned for, say, beans and peas planted in them to wind their way up the railings. Any 'patio' planters marketed as being good for growing fruit and vegetables are great for the 'no-time' gardener. Light and easy to set up, they can come in bright colours or with attractive woven willow panels to prettify them. Plastic bucket trugs are also perfect; they are readily available, cheap, light and brightly coloured, so they will cheer up the drabbest of spaces. Do bear in mind that although the container may be light, wet compost is not, so check with a structural engineer if you're at all worried about your balcony supporting the weight.

Self-watering pots

There's no getting away from it: containers dry out more quickly than garden soil does, and if you're several storeys up, the wind won't help this desiccation, but there are ways to take the hassle out of watering. Consider planters with a built-in reservoir – easily available in the shops or simple to make yourself (See Make a Simple Self-Watering Container for Free, p. 71) – which can keep even thirsty plants such as courgettes and tomatoes content for several days before having to be topped up.

Timers of the essence

If you have easy access to a water supply, a simple automatic watering system is a fantastic help. The most basic version is probably a timer fitted to your outside tap which is connected to a plastic tube with drippers coming off it at intervals of your choosing. This means you can direct these little drippers into your pots. Simply set the timer to come on for five or ten minutes twice a day and your plants won't need you nearly as much.

Mulch it

Another way to cut down on watering is to mulch the surface of the compost when you first plant up a container. This simply means spreading on a thin layer of well-rotted manure, garden compost, shingle, pebbles or bark chippings so water cannot evaporate as quickly from the compost. You can use shredded paper, sheets of newspaper, plastic or grass clippings too, but shingle is ideal on a balcony or roof since it looks attractive and won't blow away. To get the very best start, water the compost well before you first sprinkle the shingle on.

Crystal clear

Another handy watering tip, when planting in smaller containers such as hanging baskets, is to mix in a handful of water-retaining gel or crystals. These swell up, absorbing the water, and then slowly release it into the compost.

10 best easy crops

If you're short on time and expertise, the delicious crops – or groups of crops – listed here are a great place to start. The plants are relatively low-maintenance and their produce truly does taste better than the stuff you can buy in the shops. You can sow these from seed, but for a really easy life buy plug plants from garden centres or online suppliers, plant them straight out into their final growing positions and leave them to romp away happily.

Tomatoes

However little time you think you have, you have time to grow tomatoes and no summer would be complete without the scent of tomato plants on the air. Grow a pot of basil near them and you can wrap a leaf around a juicy cherry 'Sungold', then pop the whole package into your mouth, or impress your friends with purply 'Black Krim' or stripy 'Tigerella'.

From tiny cherry tomatoes so sweet you'll be eating handfuls from the plant to big, Italian beefsteak varieties, tomatoes come in all shapes and colours. Buy plants in early summer and plant them straight out. Alternatively, grow them from seed in mid-spring, sowing them about ½cm deep in 9cm pots on a sunny windowsill, turning the seedlings regularly so they don't grow crooked towards the light. Once all risk of frost has passed, plant them outside in a sunny, sheltered spot away from winds (these plants need the heat to ripen well) and feed them every fortnight from flowering onwards with a high-potash feed such as organic liquid seaweed or an organic tomato feed.

3 easy ways...

There are three types of tomato available (with many varieties of each) and each type is suited to slightly different growing methods. The type you choose depends on what container you want to grow your plants in.

Bushes need no support and grow only 30cm or so high so are best suited to a large window box or pot. A 30cm-diameter pot will take one bush, while a large window box should fit two. The upside is that there's no tying in to supports or pinching out of sideshoots; the downside is that all the tomatoes ripen at once. For bush varieties consider 'Red Alert', 'Maskotka', 'Garden Pearl', or 'Principe Borghese', which is a mini plum.

Tumbling forms trail over the edge of containers, so are perhaps best in hanging baskets. Good varieties include the prolific '100s and 1000s', and 'Tumbling Tom'.

Cordons grow tall, need supports and are best grown in a large pot or growing bag. The tomatoes ripen in stages all summer and right into autumn, so you can get a continuous harvest out of a small space. Good cordon varieties include the sweet, orange cherry tomato 'Sungold', classic red cherry 'Gardener's Delight', 'Ferline' and purply 'Black Krim'.

A 30cm-diameter pot will take up to four cordon tomatoes grown up a teepee of bamboo canes. Grow bags are an easy option – and if you can find a double-depth bag, so much the better.

Either buy metal supports or site your bag at the foot of your balcony railings or trellis and tie the plants in as they grow. Pinch out any sideshoots that form in the joint between the main stem and leaves to channel the plant's energy into fruit production. When the plant has formed six trusses of tomatoes – usually in late summer – pinch out the top of the plant just above a leaf. If you don't do this, the plant will keep growing upwards, producing fruit that won't have a chance to ripen before the weather gets colder.

Easy tip

When planting tomatoes in a grow bag, don't cut out the whole panel as the instructions tell you to. Instead, cut three crosses in the plastic and then fold the flaps under to make holes to plant in. This means less water can evaporate from the compost, helping to cut down on watering.

First or Second
Early varieties
such as Anya
are best for
growing in pots

Salad potatoes

There's something magical about tipping out a bucket of compost onto the floor and unearthing fresh spud treasure, then boiling it and eating your crop there and then with melted butter and your own potted mint. Potatoes grown in garden soil tend to be a magnet for slugs and other pests, but those grown up high in a tub, large bucket or bag show no such signs of damage. They're generally blemish-free and gleaming – needing the barest wash under the kitchen tap to clean off the compost.

Potato leaves are a welcome fountain of lime green in the spring and can soon turn a balcony into a verdant jungle. Grow First or Second Early varieties such as 'Charlotte', 'Anya', 'Orla', 'Red Duke of York' or 'Rocket' to get early new potatoes with an earthy, just-dug flavour. You can really tell the difference.

Project

SPUDS IN A TUB

WHEN TO DO: MID-SPRING

You will need

* 1 container at least 30cm in diameter – such as a rubber trug, large plastic bucket, pot or bag (not see-through). Avoid very deep pots since the plants need sunlight to develop the tubers. If using a bag, roll the sides down when you plant the tubers, then roll them up as you earth up the growing plants – this ensures the plants always get lots of sunlight
* Crocks or polystyrene pieces
* Multipurpose compost
* Seed potatoes (a 30cm-diameter pot takes two potatoes; adjust the quantity depending on the size of your container)

How to do it

First make sure your container has drainage holes, then add a layer of crocks on the base. Add about 20cm of compost and place your potatoes, with their shoots uppermost, on the compost, before covering with another 20cm of compost. Water well. If a frost is forecast, place a couple of layers of newspaper on top for protection.

Keep the compost moist and after a few weeks the potato haulms (shoots) will break the surface. When they are about 10cm high, cover them with more compost. Keep covering them each time they're about 10cm high until they reach the top of the container. Then keep watering and feed fortnightly with a tomato feed or organic liquid seaweed fertiliser. When the potatoes flower it's a sign that the tubers are ready, but have an exploratory dig around before you tip them out; different varieties mature at different times, but First Earlies are worth investigating after about 10 weeks, Second Earlies from about 13 weeks. If you dig carefully you can harvest some potatoes while leaving the others to grow on.

French beans

A wigwam of climbing French beans, with their pretty purple or white flowers, heart-shaped leaves and twining stems, is a lovely sight on any balcony. Or why not let them climb up your balcony railings, screening your neighbours and creating a jungly wall of beans?

French beans are wonderfully prolific, particularly the climbing varieties, and are delicious eaten when they're so fresh you can snap them in half. They're happy in containers as long as they have a sunny, sheltered spot and a nice deep root run, so make sure the pot is at least 20cm deep (a hanging basket is too shallow). Grow either the dwarf sort, in which case you'll need no supports, save perhaps a few twiggy sticks, or the climbing varieties, which can clamber up a wigwam, trellis, or balcony railings.

Start sowing French beans about 5cm deep from late spring and, if space allows, have at least two containers on the go, resowing the second when the initial batch form their first true leaves. Or sow a new handful of beans every fortnight up to late summer, so that you keep a good supply of beans going right up to mid-autumn. Either sow in small pots inside and transplant them when they're about 10cm tall, or sow direct into larger containers. A mixed sowing of green, purple and yellow beans makes a fabulous display when they're growing at full steam. Good climbing varieties include 'Blue Lake', 'Cobra', yellow 'Neckargold' and purple 'Blauhilde'. For dwarf varieties try 'Safari', 'Tendergreen', 'Purple Teepee' (purple) or yellow 'Rocquencourt'.

Sow dwarf French beans about 15cm apart and climbing varieties about 10cm apart around the base of a wigwam or other support they can climb up. Place them in a really warm, sheltered position, keep well watered and feed every week with a high-potash liquid feed such as seaweed or wormery feed once they start flowering. In the early stages, watch out for slugs and snails. Later, beans can attract blackfly, which can be squirted off with a jet of water or sprayed with organic insecticidal soft-soap solution. Pick the beans before the seeds inside start to bulge out of the sides of the pod. Keep picking and the plants will produce more beans.

Keep picking French beans and they will produce more pods

Salad for all seasons

Salad leaves are perhaps the easiest crops to grow on a balcony, and even a small space should provide you with fresh, springy leaves all summer long. Salad plants and containers make excellent companions – from large pots to window boxes and hanging baskets. Salad leaves are shallow-rooted, so they don't mind restricted root space; are fast-growing, so you can pack in several crops a year; and come in a glorious range of colours and textures, so they look as beautiful as any flower-packed alternative. There's something undeniably satisfying about snipping off a few fresh leaves to put in a sandwich or make a quick side salad, and you shouldn't be troubled by slugs and snails when growing them up high.

There's no reason to stop growing salad when summer ends – plenty of lettuce varieties, and other salad leaves, are hardy enough to grow outside over winter. In summer, though, the key with lettuces in small containers is regular watering, since any lettuce under stress will bolt (run to flower and turn bitter) and hanging baskets and window boxes need particular attention to stop them drying out.

If you are after mature lettuces, an average 30cm-diameter pot will hold around five. The loose-leaved, open varieties work particularly well, brimming over the edges in an irresistible frou-frou froth. Try mixing burgundy-leaved Lollo Rosso with acid-green Lollo Bianco or oak-leaf varieties, with their pretty, scalloped leaves. Crunchy little Cos lettuces, such as 'Little Gem', 'Pinokkio' and 'Tom Thumb', are also delicious, their upright habit best suiting a window box or pot.

For mature lettuces, the easiest way to grow them is probably to sow them in small pots (inside from early to late spring, outside throughout the summer) and then transplant them when the lettuces have six leaves. To harvest them, cut off individual leaves with scissors or a knife from around the edge of the plant, leaving the centre intact. This way the lettuce will keep growing and you can be taking delicious crisp leaves from one lettuce for weeks.

Baby leaves are ideal for small containers because you can grow them close together and get up to three crops from the plants before you have to resow. These baby leaves are produced by simply growing regular lettuce seeds close together and harvesting them when the leaves are small. Just sprinkle a mixture of lettuce seeds on the surface of the compost in your container, barely cover them with compost and water well. When the seedlings sprout, thin them to 5cm apart. Start harvesting when the leaves reach a size you'd feel like eating – snipping the plants off to just above the smallest new leaf. They will resprout a couple of times.

Winter salad crops

Mizuna is a serrated oriental leaf that is particularly hardy. Sow in late summer for leaves from late autumn right through to late spring. Eaten small, the leaves are rather like rocket, while larger leaves work well in stir-fries. Mibuna is similar, though the leaves are less serrated in shape.

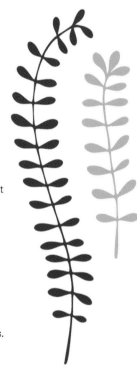

GOOD LETTUCE VARIETIES TO SOW
from spring to mid-summer

* Red and Green Oak Leaf
* Lollo Biondo
* Lollo Rosso
* Red and Green Salad Bowl
* Cos lettuces, like 'Little Gem', 'Pinokkio' or 'Tom Thumb'
* Lobjoits Cos
* Cocarde

from mid-summer to mid-autumn

* 'Red Sails'
* 'Merveille des Quatre Saisons'
* 'Valdor'
* 'Winter Density'
* 'Black Seeded Simpson'
* 'Reine de Glace'

Mustard leaves are wonderful over winter, as they are super-hardy, perky and frilly in pots and also pretty in salads. They are best picked small for salads because large leaves can be blow-your-head-off peppery, but if you do end up with monster leaves, try them finely sliced in a fiery Thai-style beef salad or stir-fry them to take the edge off their flavour. 'Red Giant' and 'Red Frills' bring a lovely burgundy colour to pots over winter and spring, while 'Golden Streaks' has delicate, feathery leaves and when picked small tastes rather like new potatoes. Sow in late summer for crops through the winter until late spring.

Winter purslane gives a crunch to winter and spring salads, with mild-flavoured, succulent stems and leaves and pretty, little, white, star-shaped flowers. Sow the tiny seeds direct as thinly as you can in late summer. Winter purslane self-sows readily, so if you don't weed too vehemently you may end up with it coming back every year.

Other salads for containers

Salad doesn't stop with lettuce, of course, and when you start growing your own, a whole world of delicious, crunchy alternatives opens up.

Radishes are so easy to grow – and so fast to mature – that it would be a real shame not to include them in your edible balcony. They can take as little as a month to go from seed to plate, adding a welcome peppery crunch to a leafy salad. A pinch of seeds sown every couple of weeks will keep you in radishes all summer long. 'Cherry Belle' is a classic red round variety, while the pretty, long 'French Breakfast' has a white tip and is perfect for slicing. 'Bright Lights' will give you multi-coloured radishes, in yellow, purple and red.

Sow radish seeds about 1cm deep and 3cm apart in any container – they will be happy in window boxes or hanging baskets as well as in larger pots.

Rocket is a peppery must-have, and you can eat fresh rocket leaves all year round if you grow it yourself. Seeds are best sown direct into the container you want to grow them in, thinly, and barely covered with compost. Wild rocket, with its serrated, sword-like leaves, is best sown from mid-spring to mid-summer, while salad rocket, milder-flavoured and hardy enough to grow over winter, should be sown from mid-summer to mid-autumn. Both types will grow in sun or partial shade and are happy in containers (though wild rocket will not be happy in something as shallow as a hanging basket). Keep plants well watered or they may bolt (run to seed). Fast-growing rocket can be snipped just above the smallest new leaf and it will resprout a couple of times before needing to be resown.

Spinach is a wonderfully versatile container crop, since you can either eat the leaves raw when young in salads or steamed when they are more mature. It will grow in any container, although in small containers it's best to harvest it as baby leaves. Sow seed thinly, 3cm deep, from early to late spring and again in the autumn for pickings all year round. Thin newly emerged seedlings to about 7cm apart.

Perpetual spinach is a great beginner's choice as it keeps producing leaves for months on end – try 'Popeye'. Other spinach varieties to try include 'Bordeaux', with its striking, purple stems. In the summer, spinach is happiest in the shade, while winter crops benefit from as much sun as possible. Keep it well watered, as spinach hates drying out, and harvest by picking individual outer leaves.

Chard, picked small and eaten raw, makes a nice salad alternative to spinach. If you choose 'Bright Lights' or 'Rainbow' chard it also has attractive multicoloured stems. Sow and grow as for spinach.

Buckler's leaf sorrel adds a delicious, citrusy tang to salads. Sow seeds direct into window boxes, hanging baskets or pots from spring to mid-summer and thin the seedlings to about 5cm apart.

Corn salad (lamb's lettuce or mache) is a lovely, mild-flavoured, rosette-forming salad leaf that is particularly valuable during the cold months since autumn sowings can be harvested in early spring. Sow thinly, 1cm deep, direct into pots or window boxes from spring to autumn. Thin seedlings to about 10cm apart.

Pea tips give you a wonderfully succulent addition to the salad bowl with an unmistakable fresh pea taste. The curly tendrils look pretty on the plate, too. If you are growing peas for shoots, sow the seeds as for normal peas (see p. 88), but more thickly – as close as 1cm apart. Using a packet of dried green peas from a food shop is the cheapest way to do this. You should be able to cut each plant two or three times.

Sunflower sprouts have a refreshingly nutty crunch and can take less than a week to go from seed to plate. Buy a packet of dried seeds from a food shop and sow them thickly, ½cm deep. Harvest the seedlings when they are about a centimetre tall and before they have their second (rather bitter) set of leaves. You can grow sunflower seedlings outside from mid-spring to mid-autumn – the rest of the year you can grow them inside on a sunny window sill.

Strawberries

We've all despaired as the supermarket strawberries we bought with great optimism slump from rock-hard acidity to grey mould overnight. Why don't strawberries taste like they used to, we wonder? Well, grow them yourself and they will – sweet, meltingly soft and abundant, and as a bonus they'll fill your balcony with the unmistakable scent of summer. So close to hand, they're perfect for popping into your mouth as you mosey around your balcony in the morning before work, for throwing into a breakfast smoothie, or onto muesli.

If you grow strawberries yourself you can enjoy some mouthwatering varieties such as 'Mara des Bois' – which is like a delectable giant woodland strawberry – the pointy-shaped French classic 'Gariguette', 'Cambridge Favourite', 'Florence' or 'Chelsea Pensioner'. It's always fun to include some real woodland strawberries, too, with their tiny, flavour-packed fruit. And for something really different, why not try a white variety?

Strawberries thrive in hanging baskets and other containers since they have fairly shallow roots, though they do need frequent feeding with a high-potash liquid fertiliser such as a tomato food or seaweed. They also make pretty plants with their buttery yellow and white flowers and fruits trailing over the edges of pots or dangling down from hanging baskets above your head, temptingly. Strawberries are also great planted under fruit trees or other large plants, and they can even be shoehorned into the pockets of fabric shoe organisers.

You can plant strawberry plants at several times throughout the year; in late summer/early autumn they will arrive as spidery, bare roots which can be planted for a crop the following summer. Alternatively, you can buy them in spring as 'cold-stored runners' (refrigerated by the supplier to confuse them so they fruit more quickly), which will crop that summer. From spring through the summer you'll also find potted plants for sale in garden centres – check out online suppliers or visit your local garden centre.

When planting strawberries, whether bare-root or potted, make sure the crown (the pointy bit in the centre from which new leaves grow) is sitting on the surface of the compost – if it's covered, it might rot; if it's too high, it might dry out.

Strawberries will last for a couple of years in a hanging basket or smallish pot before they have to be replaced. You won't need to buy new plants; you can simply make new ones by pinning down any runners (the baby plants at the end of the long stems) to the compost until they root, then cut them off. Any runners that you don't require should be snipped off close to the main plant. At the end of the summer, when the leaves turn yellow, cut plants back to about 10cm above the crown to keep them tidy (apart from 'ever-bearing' varieties such as 'Mara des Bois', which can be left as they are).

Easy tip

The classic terracotta strawberry planter looks great in a corner and can accommodate up to 12 plants, although be warned that the lower plants will struggle to get enough water unless you can get it down to them somehow. An easy way to do this is to cut a piece of PVC piping to the height of the pot and drill several holes along its length with a household drill. Put this in the centre of the pot and pour the compost in around it, being careful not to get any in the tube, then fill the tube with shingle. When you pour water into this tube, it will seep out into the compost lower down in the pot, thus keeping moist the plants at that level.

Why don't strawberries taste like they used to, we wonder? Well, grow them yourself and they will

Herbs

Perhaps no other group of edible plants is quite as useful to the balcony gardener as herbs. With little effort you can be self-sufficient in kitchen basics such as parsley, rosemary, bay, thyme, chives, mint, coriander, sage, tarragon and even basil, and have more unusual herbs at your daily disposal too, such as lemon verbena, Thai basil and chervil. Since you usually take only a few leaves at a time when harvesting herbs, a few plants go a very long way in the kitchen, and if this didn't make them worthy enough of a place on the edible balcony, their varied scents, colours and shapes certainly will.

Don't be afraid to mix your herbs for visual effect – as well as purple and green sages, how about a mixed pot of common thyme with the bright variegated variety 'Silver Queen' and the refined lemon thyme, with its particularly delicious scent. Or you could combine curly and French parsley, or plant purple-veined sorrel, with its glossy, green leaves and purple midribs, alongside purple and green

basil. With a bit of imagination, herbs can be the most beautiful among edible plants you grow.

There are so many different uses for herbs: you can use mint to make your own tea or in tzatziki, grow basil for delicious homemade fresh pesto, have a bay leaf to hand to add to that casserole or soup, or rosemary for lamb or crunchy roast potatoes.

The following are some of the easiest herbs to grow; they can all be bought as plants and simply popped into the compost for an instant herb garden. With the exception of parsley, coriander and mint, herbs generally prefer a hot spot – many come from the warm, dry Mediterranean, after all – where the sun can encourage the fragrant oils in their leaves.

Rosemary

Buy young plants in spring and plant them up into pots at least 20cm in diameter, as these will grow fairly large over time. Choose either an upright variety such as 'Miss Jessopp's Upright' or a prostrate variety (*Rosmarinus officinalis* Prostratus Group) that will look particularly good hanging over the side of large pots – leaving space to plant other herbs in the same container. Ensure your container has decent drainage holes and fill it with multipurpose compost, ideally with a couple of handfuls of grit or sand mixed in, since these plants hate to be waterlogged. Place the pots in a sunny spot and don't overwater them. Feed after flowering with a seaweed fertiliser every three weeks.

Harvest rosemary by snipping branches back to a growing bud, rather than stripping individual leaves. This herb is perfect for throwing into a roasting pan with new potatoes and garlic, and as it's evergreen it will provide a useful screen against wind or neighbours, and provide colour on your balcony year-round.

Thyme

Bring the mellow hum of honey bees to your balcony all summer long with pots of pretty flowering thyme. Not only is the herb indispensable in the kitchen but the plants look good all year round and smell delicious too. Buy young plants in spring and plant in pots, window boxes or hanging baskets in compost with sand or grit added. Choose common thyme (*Thymus vulgaris*), variegated 'Silver Queen', which is particularly pretty, or deliciously scented lemon thyme. Place in a sunny spot and water sparingly, feeding only every month or so. After flowering, trim back the shoots to avoid the plant becoming leggy. Snip off sprigs as and when you want them and add to soups, casseroles or marinades. Surplus leaves can be dried in a cool oven and then stored in an airtight jar.

Parsley

Parsley can be sown inside in mid-spring in small pots (cover the seeds with vermiculite rather than compost), but it is much easier to buy plants – two or three plants should provide enough fresh leaves for most people. The curly sort is fine, but taste-wise French flat-leaved parsley is superior. Plant in containers of multipurpose compost and place in a partially shady spot – it will even tolerate full shade and will overwinter outside. The plants are biennial, meaning they flower in their second year, so buy or sow new plants every year for a good supply of leaves. Parsley can be picked all year round, though excess leaves can be chopped and frozen in ice-cube trays or made into herb butter.

Mint

Wonderful in drinks – from mojitos (see p. 133) to tea – added to new potatoes or chopped onto fresh strawberries, mint is a must-have for the edible balcony.

It is best to buy plants in spring. Picking your way through the vast

array of varieties available is the only difficult thing with mint. You can't go wrong with garden mint or spearmint, which are best for adding to drinks and teas, but if you want something different, Moroccan mint is great in tea, black peppermint has the strongest scent and why not try chocolate mint, orange mint or pineapple mint?

However, mint is a terrible bully and will take over any pot it's planted in, so either give it its own large pot or, if you want to mix it with other plants, cut the bottom off a plastic pot and plant the mint in that, then submerge it in a larger container with the rim just poking above soil level. Place the pot in a partially shaded position, or it will even be happy in full shade.

Mint plants die down to nothing over winter, but they will resurface in the spring. If you want leaves over winter, dig up a portion of plant in autumn, roots and all, pot it up and bring it into the house.

Basil

This is one herb to grow with abandon on your balcony, since you'll want to keep picking the leaves and a single plant can quickly become exhausted. A handful of torn leaves can transform a few tomato slices into the most elegant of salads; and, crushed with garlic and pine nuts, basil makes a quick, delicious pesto.

Aim to have about three pots of plants on the go for a good supply. Sow seeds indoors from mid-spring about ½cm deep in 10cm-diameter pots (about eight seeds per pot). Put the pots on a sunny windowsill, thin to four seedlings to each pot, then transplant outside to a sunny position in larger pots or window boxes when fear of frost is over. When the plants reach about 5cm tall, pinch out (and eat) the growing tips to encourage the plants to bush out.

Alternatively, buy plants from late spring and put them straight outside. The classic variety is 'Sweet Genovese', with lush, aromatic leaves, while purple basil is rather less robust but beautiful, and aniseedy Thai basil has lovely purple stems and is the one to add for a south Asian flavour. African basil is another to consider – a robust plant with green leaves, purple stems and spikes of violet flowers in late summer that bees adore. The great thing about this variety is that it's perennial – brought inside in early autumn, African basil will keep going all winter, ready to be popped back out in mid-spring.

Coriander

You can buy plants in spring, but it's a good idea to sow coriander seeds so you can keep a constant supply, since the plants don't resprout when cut. Choose leaf coriander since that is less likely to run to seed.

Sow as for basil (above), though don't pinch out the growing shoots and ideally add grit or sand to the compost to ensure good drainage. Coriander is happiest in sun but it will tolerate partial shade.

Snip leaves as and when you want them and add to salads, soups, curries and so on – it is particularly good in Asian dishes. If you sow a handful of seeds every couple of weeks from spring until early autumn you should have a constant supply.

Chives

Spiky clumps of chives are not only invaluable in the kitchen, whether snipped on salads or fish or transforming a potato salad to herby heaven, but they look lovely too, especially when their edible, purple pom-pom flowers are in bloom.

Either buy plants in late spring (probably the best idea until you have an established clump) or sow seeds indoors ½cm deep in 10cm diameter pots on a sunny windowsill from early spring and transplant when fear of frost is over. Chives grow well in window boxes or any container in a sunny or partially shaded spot. Harvest by snipping leaves to about 3cm from the base.

Keep plants going in the autumn by digging up a portion, repotting it, then bringing it inside. Plants left outside will disappear over winter but resurface in spring. In late spring, divide the clump and replant one half in a new pot to keep your supply growing. Over summer, if you have a surplus of leaves, freeze them chopped up either in ice-cube trays or as herb butter.

Sage

When it comes to looks, the usefully evergreen sage is an underrated herb. The purple-leaved variety in particular can be stunning when it is planted among other green herbs, or in contrast to its common green cousin – though beware, it's less hardy than the green one and less vigorous, too, so it can get swamped. They're hardy enough to withstand any but the wettest, harshest winters uncovered and will provide a dash of welcome colour over the dark months.

A little sage goes a long way, so one plant is enough for most people. Lucky, really, since these plants can grow quite large. Buy young plants in spring and pot up in multipurpose compost, ideally with a little sand or grit added. Place in a sunny spot and pick leaves as and when you want them.

Bay

A standard bay may be a bit of a cliché – the standard sentinels for Italian trattorias worldwide – but why mess with a classic when they look so good? Either buy a ready-trained one or (far cheaper) buy a couple of small ones and spend the money on really good terracotta pots for them instead. To train a bay into a lollipop shape, simply snip off any sideshoots coming off the main stem, leaving a nest of shoots at the top. Keep trimming away the side-shoots up the main stem as the plant grows, to create a ball at the top over two or three years; this just needs to be shaped a couple of times a year.

Since you'll only ever need a few leaves at a time for casseroles or soups, one bay tree is more than enough. As an evergreen, bay will also provide a useful screen over winter if you don't want to look at your neighbours, and a shaped tree will be an attractive focal point when everything else has died back.

Oregano

Oregano or marjoram is a pretty, sprawling plant that will soon trail over the edge of a pot. Its flowers are a magnet for bees and the strongly scented leaves are the mainstay of Italian and Greek cooking.

Buy plants in spring, transplant them into multipurpose compost in larger pots or window boxes and position in a warm, sunny and sheltered spot. Cut the plant back in the autumn or spring to stop it getting too woody, but it can be left to overwinter outside. Over the summer surplus leaves can be picked and dried in a cool oven, then stored in an airtight jar.

Tarragon

It may not look like much, but this delicate-fronded herb punches well above its weight in the kitchen with a gentle, aniseedy taste that is the perfect partner for chicken and fish. Make sure you buy French tarragon rather than the hardier but bitter Russian version. Buy plants in spring and place them in a sunny spot in multipurpose compost, ideally with sand or grit added to improve drainage. In the autumn, bring the whole pot inside to a sunny windowsill, since this is a tender herb that won't survive winter outside. By early spring new leaves will sprout and you can put the plant back outside when the frosts are over. Any surplus leaves produced over the summer can be chopped and frozen into herb butter.

Lemon verbena

For scent rather more than for its looks, lemon verbena should be included in any herb garden. Its rough, strap-like leaves release a delectable, sherberty-lemon tang when rubbed between your fingers and it makes the most delicious tea. Buy young plants in late spring or summer and plant out in a sunny, sheltered spot. A tender perennial, lemon verbena should be brought indoors over winter or covered with a couple of layers of horticultural fleece – surplus leaves can be trimmed and stored in an airtight container after drying in a cool oven.

Lemon verbena leaves release a delectable sherberty lemon tang and make the most delicious tea

Carrots

Homegrown carrots are in another league from the shop-bought variety. Grow them yourself and you can pick them young, crunchy and wonderfully sweet. Eat them raw, make juice from them or steam them briefly to retain their delectable sweetness. Choose early varieties such as 'Nantes' and 'Amsterdam Forcing', but if you're feeling more experimental, 'Rainbow Mix' contains purple, yellow, white and orange carrots, while ball-rooted 'Paris Market' can even grow in shallow window boxes.

Sow seeds from mid-spring, thinly and barely covered with compost, in large, fairly deep pots. If you resow a new tub every time a batch puts out its first 'true' leaves, you should have a constant supply over the summer. Carrots don't need rich soil, nor as much water as some crops, but they do need good drainage, so mix horticultural sand in with multipurpose compost (in a ratio of about 1 to 4). Once the seedlings are big enough to handle, thin them to about 5cm apart. Pull up the carrots when they have reached a decent size, usually after two or three months.

Project

Carrots and marigolds in a colourful tub

The carrots' fresh feathery leaves look beautiful with the bright orange marigolds. Rubber or plastic tub trugs with drainage holes are ideal for growing as they are light, colourful and you can easily move them around..

WHEN TO DO: SPRING

You will need
* 1 plastic tub trug or similar
* Drill with 3mm (min) drill bit
* Crocks or polystyrene pieces
* Multipurpose compost
* Horticultural sand (optional)
* 1 packet carrot seeds
* Sand for seeds
* 1 packet pot marigold seeds (*Calendula officinalis*)

How to do it
Make about 10 holes (at least 3mm in diameter) in the base of the tub using a drill. Then add a layer of polystyrene chunks or other crocks before filling the tub with a mixture of three-quarters compost to one-quarter horticultural sand, almost to the rim.

Mix your carrot seeds with a handful of dry sand and sprinkle them thinly on the surface of the compost, then ruffle the compost with your fingers so that the seeds are hidden. Make a dozen or so holes in the compost with your finger, about 1cm deep, pop a marigold seed into each and cover with compost. Water well and place in a sunny spot. Thin the carrots to about 5cm apart and eat the young thinnings raw in salads.

Courgettes, squashes and pumpkins

You'll need a large container for these rampaging beasts, but they're worth growing since they're prolific producers and will quickly fill a space with their huge, sandpapery leaves and show-off, blousy, yellow flowers.

Grow courgettes in a large pot about 45cm in diameter. Trailing varieties such as 'Black Forest' can be trained up railings and trellis, while even bush varieties such as 'Defender', 'Romanesco', round 'Eight Ball' and yellow

'Soleil' can cover some distance when they get going. 'Tuscany' is a good compact choice for smaller spaces.

Squashes and pumpkins need a big pot, too. They will sprawl everywhere, so to keep the plant tidy, either place it by balcony railings and tie it to them as it grows or push a wigwam into the centre of the container and train the plant up round it. Summer squash varieties to try include 'Sunburst', a relatively compact plant that produces masses of custard-yellow squashes that are delicious steamed and eaten whole when young. When it comes to winter squashes (hard-skinned ones that keep for months), it's best to avoid butternuts unless you live in a warm climate, since they don't ripen reliably. Instead, you can't do much better then the beautiful onion squash 'Red Kuri' (sometimes called 'Uchiki Kuri'), which is a hard-skinned, orange globe that decorates the vine like lanterns and will ripen even in a poor summer. There is also a blue-skinned version – 'Blue Kuri' – for the even more adventurous, or choose the weird and wacky, curly 'Tromboncino' or 'Spaghetti' squash, which may look nothing special on the plant – a creamy, egg-shaped fruit – but when cut open reveals pasta-like strands. Chop the squash in half and microwave it for a few minutes, then eat the flesh with plenty of butter, salt and freshly ground black pepper. Pumpkins will also grow well in a large container, but if space is restricted, try the relatively compact 'Baby Bear' for best results.

To grow courgettes, squashes and pumpkins, sow seeds on their sides and 3cm deep in small pots of multipurpose compost in mid-spring on a sunny windowsill. Alternatively, buy plants in early summer and plant them straight out. As long as they are given plenty of water – every day on hot days – and fed fortnightly with a high-potash feed such as organic liquid seaweed, courgettes, squashes and pumpkins will be happy. If you can mulch them with a 5cm layer of well-rotted manure, garden compost or wormery compost, so much the better.

Chillies

Few crops are as suited to container growing as these hot-blooded, compact plants. Even one plant on a balcony can produce enough chillies for all but the most obsessive chilliphile. From the mild 'Hungarian Hot Wax' to fiery 'Jalapeno', 'Thai Bird's Eye' and 'Etna', there are chillies for every taste, colour and shape, and as a bonus the plants are perky and cheerful and their colourful fruits look wonderfully exotic on a balcony.

Sow seeds inside in early spring in small pots, just covering them with compost, then pot them on into bigger pots if they become pot-bound. Transplant them outside in early summer once all risk of frost has passed, into a sunny, sheltered spot. Feed every fortnight from flowering with an organic liquid seaweed feed and bring back inside in mid-autumn to allow the fruits to fully ripen. Dry or freeze surplus chillies. Water sparingly over winter and the plant should sprout new leaves come spring. Mulch with wormery or garden compost and the plant can then be put outside again in late spring/early summer.

Blueberries

A couple of potted blueberry bushes are a great choice for a balcony; they're handsome plants with creamy flowers and leaves that often turn red in the autumn. Blueberries are completely hardy, so no winter protection is needed, nor do they require much care or pruning (just trim away dead branches); their only requirement is that they are planted in ericaceous (acidic) compost, which is available from all garden centres. Choose a pot at least 30cm in diameter. Ideally, blueberries prefer to be watered with rain water, although if this isn't available, tap water will do. They should be fed fortnightly once they start flowering with an organic liquid seaweed or wormery feed.

The best thing about blueberries, though, is the quantity of fruit that they produce from mid-summer right up to mid-autumn, and how delicious it is – far firmer, tarter and more aromatic than those rather mealy berries you buy in the shops. Good varieties include 'Bluecrop', 'Earliblue' and 'Sunshine Blue'.

'NO TIME' BALCONY NON-EDIBLE COMPANIONS

For low-maintenance, non-edible plants to combine with your delicious crops, consider hardy exotics such as *Cordyline australis*, *Trachycarpus fortunei* and *Phormium tenax*. You also can't go wrong with ornamental grasses such as *Miscanthus* and bamboo, or why not sow easy-flowering annuals direct into your pots in mid- to late spring? They'll die by the end of autumn, but will transform your space into a colourful bonanza for the whole summer. Nasturtiums, sunflowers, sweetpeas, cosmia, nigella (love-in-a-mist) and marigolds are all easily sown straight into pots. Mix them in with your edibles and you get the best of both worlds – lettuces with nasturtiums, sweetpeas entwined with sugar-snap peas, or sunflowers waving amidst a sea of sweetcorn are all combinations that look fantastic.

Served with a dollop of yogurt, blueberries make the ideal on-the-go breakfast

How You Make It Personal

Gardens several storeys up don't happen by accident – people put them there. It's no wonder, then, that balconies and roof gardens are often so highly individual, bringing out all your latent creativity, giving you your own domain to play with, however small. They open up a whole world of possibilities not only for the crops you grow, but the way you choose to grow them. Forget terracotta-coloured plastic pots, there are far more exciting ways to show off your edibles – some quirky, some unexpectedly beautiful and many of them completely free.

Save me: the salvaged balcony

Reclaimed, salvaged, rescued – call them what you will – so many materials that were once at the centre of domestic life are these days more likely to be found gathering dust in junk shops, architectural salvage yards or car-boot sales and history's galvanised baths, buckets, tubs, teapots and cans are a balcony gardener's treasure trove. Old tiles, bricks, clay pipes, hat stands, have a real beauty in their own right and often make surprisingly good planters. They bring a lived-in charm and individuality to any roof or balcony space, and provide humour too.

It's great fun to track down salvage items; whether it's finding the perfect twin-handled tub in a market and snapping it up for a couple of pounds to grow carrots and marigolds in, or garlanding a hat stand with hanging baskets. If the idea of spending money on reclaimed materials doesn't appeal, try the free online swap site 'freecyle' and keep your eyes out for skips – it's amazing what people throw away. After all, one man's dented kitchen colander is another man's tumbling tomato hanging basket.

Turn old junk into great plant pots

As long as you can punch or drill drainage holes in the bottom, any old container will work to grow plants in. The only real limitation is weight. Do you really want to carry a butler's sink up flights of stairs, regardless of how cute it might look planted up with herbs? The key before you buy or 'save' containers to use as plant pots is that you actually want to look at them. There's little point in going to the trouble of preparing and planting up a rusty old tin if it just ends up looking like rubbish that should be in landfill. But everyone has their own taste, and the real fun of salvage-style balconies is that they let you express yourself – so don't be afraid to experiment.

Wood is good

Old wine or fruit crates are sturdy and hardwearing and look great overflowing with salad leaves or herbs. Drawers work well, too, and are often deep enough to take large plants such as tomatoes, courgettes, aubergines or chillies.

Old wine barrels can look good and are deep enough for a fruit tree, but they are heavy, so bear this in mind. Don't underestimate the humble wicker wastepaper basket either. If you're particularly handy, you can even make planting troughs from scratch for free from old scaffolding boards or pieces of wood discarded in skips – just make sure there are drainage holes in the base and, obviously, if you are at all concerned about the weight of any container on your balcony or roof, seek advice from a structural engineer, builder or surveyor before you go ahead.

Balconies overhung by others above them will be protected from the rain, so in this situation you can use salvaged pieces that may not last long when exposed to the elements. Bookcases and dressers make perfect plant stands with much more character than those you'd get from a garden centre, planted wardrobe a1 while old chests of drawers can become fabulous planters, with staggered drawers revealing bumper crops of dwarf French beans, chard, lettuce or strawberries. Look out, too, for old wooden hat stands or umbrella racks that can be useful for growing climbing plants up, such as beans, or that you can hang baskets of strawberries and tumbling tomatoes from.

Any wooden container will eventually rot when filled with damp compost, but they'll last much longer if you paint them with a natural non-toxic preserving oil such as Danish oil and strengthen their corners with metal corner braces, otherwise the corner joints are prone to coming apart. Don't use varnish as this won't allow the wood to breathe and if water does get in it can't get out, so it will rot the wood. It's also a good idea to line any wooden boxes or drawers with plastic before you plant them up in order to prolong the life of the wood. Make sure there are generous holes in the plastic aligned with those you've drilled in the base so that excess water can drain away easily.

Metal containers

Vintage galvanised domestic containers such as old laundry tubs, cattle troughs, baths, buckets and trays make great planters, with their mellow, silvery colour bringing real softness to a space and catching the sunlight beautifully. They're much lighter than they look, retain moisture well (since water can't evaporate through the sides) and come in lovely shapes, often with attractive handles. Of course, because they're galvanised they don't rust either, so they are ideal for using outside. Drill holes in the base (or punch them using a nail) and put a layer of broken crocks or polystyrene down before adding the compost. A galvanised twin-handled tub planted up with carrots and marigolds is a lovely sight. Or how about silver-leaved thyme in an old teapot?

Even rusty buckets with holes in can look fabulous lined up on a bench filled with herbs or flowers. Enamel bread bins and other vintage kitchen containers, with their big retro lettering, add a nice humorous touch, and wrought-iron shelving or racks can come into service as quirky climbing frames for squashes and beans.

10 not-in-the-shops crops

Creating a highly individual balcony garden doesn't have to stop with the containers you choose; one of the best things about growing your own fruit and vegetables is that you can include weird and wonderful crops you can't easily buy. And what's the best news about unusual edibles? Just because you don't see them very often it doesn't mean they're difficult to grow.

Buckler's leaf sorrel

This tangy, little-known salad leaf is great for growing in containers, where you can appreciate its delicate, shield-like leaves close up. Sow seed directly into multipurpose compost in pots, window boxes or hanging baskets in late spring, then eat the young leaves raw in salads, to which its sharp, lemony flavour brings a wonderful bite.

'Bright Lights' chard

You won't see this pretty spinach-like crop (right) in the shops because it doesn't store well, but since you'll be eating it from your balcony within minutes of picking, that really doesn't matter. Large, green leaves are held aloft on vivid red, yellow, orange and purple stems. Eat the mature leaves steamed and dotted with plenty of butter and a little garlic, cooking the stems for longer than the leaves – they're delicious in a gratin.

For mature leaves, sow seeds thinly 1cm deep from mid-spring in a medium–large container (at least 30cm in diameter) and then thin seedlings to about 20cm apart. You can also eat the baby leaves raw in salads; if you want baby leaves, sow seeds 1cm deep and

about 1cm apart direct into medium–large containers from mid-spring to late summer, then harvest them by cutting just above the smallest new leaf when the plants are about 10cm tall. For a slightly less visually impressive variety of chard, but one that tastes arguably even better, go for Swiss or silver chard, with deep green leaves and white stems.

Wild strawberries

Smaller than their cultivated cousins and with a more intense, aromatic taste, wild strawberries are just perfect to be enjoyed as you wander round with a watering can. Happy in hanging baskets, window boxes and pots, they're very low-maintenance as they don't send out as many runners as the larger, cultivated kinds of fruit. Buy as plants from spring to autumn and allow two or three plants to a 30cm-diameter pot. Feed every fortnight from flowering onwards with a high- potash feed such as liquid seaweed.

'Tromboncino' or 'Serpente' squash

This climbing squash (see above, far right) has light green, courgette-like fruits that grow in curly shapes. It looks stunning grown over a pergola or railings where the fruits can hang down. Sow in mid-spring in small pots inside, then transplant in early summer, giving it a good support to climb up and about 20cm space all around it. Once the first fruits form, feed every fortnight with a high-potash feed such as liquid seaweed. Eat the fruits, which are produced right up to mid-autumn, as you would courgettes.

Purple, orange and stripy tomatoes

Perhaps the sweetest tomato you can grow, the orange cherry tomato 'Sungold' is a must-have for any edible balcony. 'Black Krim' is a larger purple tomato with a crisp, salty-sweet taste. The stripes of 'Tigerella' start off green and then turn red and yellow as the tomato ripens. All are no harder to grow than regular red tomatoes, but far, far more interesting. (See p. 30 for sowing and growing instructions.)

Blue potatoes

'Vitelotte', 'Congo', 'Salad Blue' – some of the old, unusual potato varieties you can buy these days sound so romantic you'll want to plant them on the basis of their names alone. From purple to blue to deepest black, these potatoes make real talking points and have a dense, nutty flavour that is just delicious when roasted. (See p. 33 for planting and growing instructions.)

Rainbow carrots

Yellow, white, orange, purple and red carrots are a bit more interesting than a plateful of mere orange; and they're reputed to be healthier for you, too. Most seed suppliers now sell a multicoloured mix. (See p. 48 for sowing and growing instructions.)

Borlotti beans

A real flavour of Italy; grow these like any climbing bean (see, p. 34), in a large pot with support nearby so that they can clamber high, showing off their stunning red-and-green-flecked pods. Inside the speckled beans are just as pretty as the pods and delicious eaten fresh with coriander and Parmesan or dried for use in soups.

Sow seeds in late spring about 2cm deep in multipurpose compost. Sow directly into a pot, aiming for about 12 seeds in a 30cm-diameter pot, and provide a wigwam or other climbing support for the developing seedlings. Harvest the beans in early autumn when the pods are slightly green with a streaky red and cream skin underneath.

Tayberries

A delicious cross between a blackberry and a raspberry, this unusual cane fruit can be grown in a large container (at least 40cm diameter) and the stems tied into supports as they grow. When each cane has fruited, simply cut it down to soil level and it will regrow next year. Harvest in mid- summer when the fruits are dark and sweet.

positioned in sun or partial shade, and feed only once a year in spring with garden compost, well-rotted manure or liquid seaweed. Harvest the berries in late autumn. A row of these bushes would make a good evergreen hedge to block out neighbours.

A real flavour of Italy, borlotti beans have stunning red- and green-flecked pods

Chilean guava

An evergreen shrub from the myrtle family, this looks a bit like a box bush but has the bonus of wonderful berries that ripen in the autumn. Reputedly Queen Victoria's favourite fruit, these red berries taste rather like a peppery strawberry, or strawberry Space Dust – that explosive, sherberty childhood sweet of years ago.

Plant young plants in ericaceous compost in a medium container (they like to feel snug around the roots)

Project

PEAS AND SWEETPEAS IN A WICKER BASKET

Wicker wastepaper baskets make ideal light planters with a nice rustic look. Peas grow well in a container like this since they have relatively deep roots and, when paired with sweetpeas you get a wonderful riot of scent, flowers and pods. Pick the pea pods and sweetpea flowers regularly to keep both plants producing more. The green, hairy, inedible pods of the sweetpea are easy to tell apart from the edible pods of the pea, but sowing purple-podded mangetout makes sure there's no room for uncertainty. At the end of the season, cut the plants off at the base, leaving the roots in the soil – they will add nitrogen to the soil. You can then replant with salad for a late crop.

WHEN TO DO: MID-SPRING TO EARLY SUMMER
You will need

* ✳ 1 wicker wastepaper basket
* ✳ 1 black bin bag or other piece of plastic
* ✳ Multipurpose compost
* ✳ A handful of twiggy sticks, such as prunings, at least 36cm long canes – don't use bamboo; they're too slippery and the peas can't cling on
* ✳ A handful of sweetpea seedlings
* ✳ 1 packet of pea seeds (a dwarf variety is best for containers – purple-podded are ideal)

How to do it

Line the basket with the plastic, then make three holes in it at the bottom. Fill with compost almost to the top. Push the sticks into the compost – there's no need to tie them into a wigwam shape. Plant the seedlings, then push the pea seeds into the compost with your finger up to the second finger joint (about 5cm) and push the compost back over the holes. Water well and place in a sheltered, sunny or partially shaded spot.

When the peas emerge, encourage their tendrils to cling onto the twiggy sticks, and perhaps snip off a few tips to use raw in salads, then leave the majority to grow to maturity. Feed every week with a liquid seaweed feed once the peas start flowering.

If you can't find twiggy sticks to grow the peas up, position the basket near your balcony railings and encourage them to climb by tying lengths of string horizontally between the railings.

Retro containers from breadbins to teapots make quirky planters

Project

BEETS IN A BREAD BIN

Enamel flour and bread bins were used in kitchens until fairly recently, but these days you're more likely to find them in junk shops, flea markets or 'retro' kitchen stores. Their colours and vintage text make them fun, unusual containers, and they're easy to adapt to growing plants – deep enough for beetroot, carrots, herbs, salad, strawberries, tumbling tomatoes or dwarf French beans. Smaller enamel kitchen tins, such as those for sugar, coffee and tea, make nice pots for compact herbs such as basil, chives and coriander.

WHEN TO DO: MID-SPRING TO MID-SUMMER

You will need

* A household drill
* An enamel kitchen container such as a bread or flour bin
* Crocks, polystyrene or shingle
* Multipurpose compost
* 1 packet of beetroot seeds – a 'baby' variety such as 'Pablo' or 'Pronto' is ideal

How to do it

Drill several holes at least 3mm in diameter in the base of the bin, then add a layer of crocks, shingle or chunks of polystyrene to improve drainage. Fill almost to the top with compost. Sow the beetroot seed 5cm apart, pushing the seeds in to a depth of 2cm. Back-fill the holes using your fingers and water well. Place in a sunny sheltered spot.

When the beets are golf-ball-sized, pull them up and roast them whole for delicious salads, especially when teamed with homegrown new potatoes and baby broad beans.

Easy tip

Beetroot leaves are delicious raw in salads. Try snipping off a few now and then while the beetroots are maturing – taking leaves won't affect the plant as long as you leave a good few to grow on.

Project

TOP DRAWER: COLOURFUL COURGETTES

Old chests of drawers don't have to end up on the tip: you can rescue the drawers and make them into lovely free wooden planters deep enough to grow most fruit and vegetables in. Apply a coat of brightly coloured exterior gloss paint and you'll find they scrub up rather well. Leave the handles on for the full effect.

Courgettes are a good choice to plant in drawers since they're hungry, sprawling plants that benefit from the space. Even so, a bush variety is ideal since it won't sprawl quite so much. Try 'Tuscany', 'Firenze', 'Midnight', the vivid yellow 'Soleil', or the round 'Eight Ball'. If in doubt, look for a variety recommended for containers. Since it may take a while for the courgette to fill the drawer, you might want to make the most of the available growing space with a quick crop of radishes.

WHEN TO DO: LATE SPRING TO EARLY SUMMER

You will need

* ❋ 1 wooden drawer from a chest of drawers or dresser
* ❋ Exterior gloss paint – a bright, cheerful colour works well
* ❋ A paintbrush
* ❋ A household drill
* ❋ Plastic lining (optional – just a precaution as you don't know what chemicals have been used to treat the drawer and you may not want these to leach into the compost)
* ❋ Crocks, shingle or polystyrene chunks
* ❋ Multipurpose compost
* ❋ 1 courgette plant – ideally a compact variety, such as 'Tuscany' or the round 'Eight Ball'
* ❋ 1 packet of radish seeds, such as 'French Breakfast' (optional)

How to do it

Paint the surfaces of the drawer that you will see and leave to dry. Turn the drawer over and drill about 10 holes at least 3mm in diameter in the base of the drawer, then turn back over. Place the drawer where you want it to stay – a sunny spot is essential. If you're lining the base with plastic, pierce holes in it so that they align with the holes you have drilled in the wood. Add a layer of crocks or other drainage material to the bottom of the drawer and fill it with compost.

Plant the courgette, then sow some radish seeds (if using) in the bare area about 1cm deep and water well. Feed the courgette every week from flowering with liquid seaweed and pick the fruits when they are about 10cm long. You can also eat the flowers; them off, wash, then stuff with ricotta and dip in a light batter before deep-frying them.

For any container a compact variety of courgette is best, such as yellow 'Soleil', left

Project

HATS OFF FOR LUNCH

This quirky salvage project is perfect for a small balcony since it takes up barely any space in a sunny corner but can support masses of plants. Not only can you hang baskets or other containers filled with strawberries, tomatoes, salad or herbs from the hooks, but the central stem is perfect for supporting climbing beans or cucumbers – and all in the space it takes to hang your sun hat. Many of us have an old coat/hat stand somewhere, and if you don't, you might well know someone who does and who would be delighted to get rid of it. Or try 'freecycle'.

WHEN TO DO: LATE SPRING–EARLY SUMMER

You will need

- ✳ 1 hat stand
- ✳ 2 large (at least 30cm-diameter) pots
- ✳ Multipurpose compost

Runner beans will soon climb up and cover hatstands and other structures

- ✳ 2 cucumber plants (ideally a 'mini' variety, such as 'La Diva' or 'Vega')
- ✳ 10 climbing bean plants – either French (try 'Blue Lake', yellow 'Rocquencourt' or purple 'Blauhilde') or runner beans (such as 'Painted Lady' or 'Scarlet Emperor')
- ✳ Garden twine or string
- ✳ 2 × 30cm-diameter hanging baskets or other containers
- ✳ 3 strawberry plants – try 'Mara des Bois', 'Cambridge Favourite' or 'Gariguette'
- ✳ 1 tumbling tomato plant – such as '100s and 1000s' or 'Tumbler'
- ✳ 4 smaller hanging containers
- ✳ Assorted salad and/or herb seedlings

How to do it

Put the hat stand in a sheltered, sunny spot – a corner is ideal as you don't want it toppling over in the wind. If it still seems a bit rickety, lay heavy stones against the base or attach to the wall with a chain and wrap it round it, but the large pots should wedge it in pretty well anyway.

Fill the two large pots with compost and place them at the base of the stand. Plant one with the cucumbers and one with the beans, then tie several lengths of string from the top ring of the hat stand down to the bottom. These will give the plants something to climb up in addition to the central column.

Plant one hanging basket with strawberries, the other with the tomato, and hang them at the top of the hat stand. Plant up the smaller containers with the salad and herbs and hang those up too.

When the cucumber plant has five leaves, pinch out the growing tip to encourage it to branch out, then tie these branches in to the strings or hat stand itself. When the beans and cucumber reach the top of the hat stand, pinch out the growing shoots and let them bush out. Keep well watered and, if possible, mulch the beans and cucumbers with a 5cm layer of garden or worm compost during the summer. Give the tomatoes and strawberries a fortnightly dose of liquid seaweed feed and the beans and salad a feed every three weeks or so.

Takeaway coffee cups and yogurt pots make ideal seedling starter homes

The recycled balcony

Have a look around your kitchen; chances are there are dozens of tubs, boxes, bottles and tins that you throw away every week, destined for landfill or your recycling centre. Venture into your garage, your loft or the back of your cupboards and you'll find unloved or imperfect items you never quite got round to throwing out – shower racks that don't stick to the tiles any more, or hanging shoe organisers you never used. Yet why spend money on expensive and generic pots from the garden centre when, with a bit of imagination, you can turn much of this household detritus into ingenious planters – from a hanging bottle herb garden to self-watering planters or pockets of strawberries to sling over your railings?

The only rule is, there are no rules – as long as it's recycled. If you don't have anything suitable lying around the house, try asking at friendly local delis for things they are throwing out – old food containers or olive oil tins are often quite stylishly designed. Greengrocers are usually more than happy to shift some of their wooden fruit-packing boxes (line them with plastic first and don't expect them to last more than a season), and fishmongers their polystyrene crates (these are particularly good for a balcony as they are so light). Plastic storage boxes with lids are also ideal – if they have wheels, so much the better, since large ones will become heavy when filled with damp compost. The addition of the lid turns them into handy cloches to protect young spring seedlings, too.

Once you start looking at recycled objects with your balcony garden in mind, it becomes surprisingly addictive and all the more satisfying when you know you're giving a new lease of life to objects otherwise destined for the bin. And don't be afraid to be eccentric: in an experiment in Chicago in 1997, 446kg of vegetables were grown in 38 children's paddling pools.

SAVE MONEY ON SEEDLINGS

Don't feel you have to spend money on pots or module trays when starting off seedlings – plastic fruit punnets, yoghurt pots and the base of cut-down plastic bottles all work equally well. Just make sure you punch generous holes in the base – or, even better, the bottom of the sides – first. Fruit punnets are particularly good since they already have ventilation holes, so there's no need to punch drainage holes. They also often come with clear plastic lids, which make them instant free cloches for starting off tender seeds such as chillies, sweet peppers and tomatoes.

A COLANDER OF TOMATOES AND NASTURTIUMS

Why use a boring traditional hanging basket when this is just as easy and much more original? This is the perfect use for old kitchen colanders hidden at the back of the cupboard, but if you don't have one, pick up a charmingly bashed-in vintage one at a junkyard, street market or boot sale, or why not buy a modern one in a vivid, sherberty colour? It's still likely to be cheaper than a hanging basket.

This combination of nasturtiums and tomatoes and is fabulously colourful – with the orange flowers clashing with the scarlet fruits to brilliant effect.

WHEN TO DO: LATE SPRING TO MID-SUMMER

You will need

* 1 colander
* Piece of plastic, such as an old compost bag or a bin bag for lining the colander
* Multipurpose compost
* 1 tumbling tomato plant, such as '100s and 1000s' or 'Tumbling Tom'
* 3 nasturtium plants or a handful of nasturtium seeds
* Strong string/rope, such as drapery cord

How to do it

Line the colander with the plastic, making a large hole at the bottom so the water is free to drain straight out of the bottom but can't get out of the sides. Fill the colander with compost, then plant the tomato in the centre and the nasturtiums around the edge (if growing the latter from seed, push in about five seeds, 2cm deep at even intervals, and thin later to three plants). Water well. Hang up with the string over your balcony railings or any other suitable support. If none is available, fix a hanging-basket bracket to the wall and hang from that.

Keep well watered and mulched with garden or worm compost. Once the tomato's fruits are pea-sized, feed every week with a tomato food or liquid seaweed fertiliser.

Make your own gentle watering can

Seedlings are easily drowned if they are subjected to a gush of water from a watering-can spout or tap. You can transform a plastic bottle into the perfect watering device for small seedlings by piercing lots of little holes in the lid with a bradawl or any other small spike. Fill the bottle, then squeeze it for a gentle shower that will water your plants without upsetting them.

wet compost gets very heavy and you don't want the pouches to break. These can be used as stand-alone pots elsewhere on your balcony – larger ones could easily house a sweet pepper, aubergine or tomato plant. Depending on how many rows your organiser has, you can end up with as many as three containers.

WHEN TO DO: MID-SPRING
You will need
❋ An over-door fabric shoe-organiser
❋ Scissors
❋ Multipurpose compost
❋ Plug plants of lettuce, strawberries, French beans, chillies or herbs – one for each pocket
❋ Water-retaining gel (optional)

How to do it
Cut off the bottom part of the organiser if necessary, leaving only the top row of pockets. Fill each pocket half-full with compost, mixing in water-retaining gel (to the packet's instruction) if you're using them, to retain moisture in the compost. Tap the pockets down gently on the floor to settle them. Plant your plug plants and fill in with more compost. Water well and hang up.

Salads and shade-tolerant herbs such as parsley, coriander and mint are happy in partial shade, but strawberries, tomatoes, other herbs and dwarf French beans require full sun.

Project
DO MY HERBS GO WITH MY SHOES?

This is a cute, attractive way to grow herbs, salad, strawberries or chillies in a small space without even having to get out the power drill. Many of us have a fabric hanging shoe-organiser lurking in the back of a cupboard – or pick one up cheap at a discount store. An 'over-door' organiser is ideal because it comes with hooks that you can simply slot over balcony railings, fences, walls or trellis. A dark colour is best since light material tends to show stains from the wet compost over time.

Depending on how long the organiser is, you may want to cut off the bottom row of pockets –

Project
MAKE A SIMPLE, SELF-WATERING CONTAINER FOR FREE

We've all been there – you're on your way back home after a long weekend away and you suddenly remember with a sick feeling of dread that your tomato plants haven't been watered for three days. You return to find them wilted and very upset indeed. However, if you make one of these ingenious self-watering planters, long guilt-free weekends will be yours once again.

These containers have a built-in reservoir of water so the plants can take up moisture through their roots for several days before the reservoir needs to be refilled. You may not want to make lots of them, but if you have particularly thirsty plants, such as courgettes, tomatoes or aubergines, they're ideal. There are plenty of more complicated versions of this system, but the one described here is beautifully simple and easy to make with things you'll probably have lying around the house.

WHEN TO DO: ANY TIME, THOUGH PLANT UP FROM EARLY SPRING TO LATE SUMMER

You will need
* Scissors
* 1 medium (around 12cm-diameter) plastic plant pot
* 1 large planter – a plastic storage box with holes drilled in the bottom is perfect
* 1 large plastic bottle – a 5-litre one is ideal, with lid on
* 1 length of pipe about the same height as your planter – plastic garden hose is fine; a rigid plastic water pipe is ideal
* Multipurpose compost
* Funnel (optional)

How to do it

With your scissors, cut about a dozen holes in the sides of the plastic plant pot, then cut a hole in the side of the bottle so that the plant pot fits snugly into it. Push the plant pot into the hole as far as you can, making sure the bottom is not touching the side of the bottle. Lay the bottle on its side on the base of the planter with the pot uppermost. This will act as your reservoir.

Next to the pot, cut a smaller hole in the bottle just big enough for the pipe to fit into and push it in. Fill the plant pot with compost, pressing it down firmly. Then fill the reservoir bottle by pouring water into the pipe (a funnel makes this much easier). Finally, fill the planter with compost as normal and plant your plants. You can keep topping up the reservoir via the pipe every week or so.

Inspiration
A REAL LITTLE FIND

If the front windows overflowing with a froth of tomato plants don't give the first hint that Mark Ridsdill Smith's Victorian terrace in north London is in the grip of a growing obsession, a visit to his tiny first-floor balcony out the back (see p. 77) certainly confirms it. In a space no more than 3 × 2m, this avid grower has created an ingenious and vibrant kitchen garden, packed with beans, salads, courgettes, herbs and tomatoes.

Recycled and found items are everywhere, from the wooden planters handmade by Mark from floor boards he picked up in skips on the street to two halves of a child's plastic hula hoop co-opted into a handy frame to protect early crops. Rainwater is channelled from the roof into a plastic olive barrel and then, regulated by a stopcock, travels along plastic piping through the line of linked wooden planters where it tops up reservoirs inside them. Put simply, the balcony waters itself. All Mark has to do is sit back and pick his lush red and green lettuces and enjoy looking at the marigold flowers nestling among his runner beans.

Project
CREATE A SALAD CASCADE

If you're after a more minimal look for your vertical crops, why not grow salad and herbs in lengths of plastic guttering and attach them to the wall? It's a fantastic use of space for small urban balconies and looks sleek and modern – particularly if you plant crops that cover the guttering as they grow, giving the appearance of floating in mid-air. Crops harvested when very young such as pea shoots and sunflower shoots are ideal, while lettuce, spinach, chard and rocket, grown as baby leaves, also work well. Salad onions and herbs such as basil and coriander, harvested when small, are happy growing in this way too. Guttering is good for growing crops on a shady or partially shaded wall, since the small volume of compost will dry out quickly in a hot spot.

To start crops off super-early, sow seeds in the guttering inside in early spring and then hang it up outside when risk of frost is over.

Alternatively, you could start it off outside and cover the salad cascade with a sheet of protective plastic if you're worried about frost. If you don't want to use seed, simply buy small plug plants and pop them in in mid-spring.

One of the beauties of this system is that any excess water drips down into the gutter below, so you don't waste any. And if you water carefully, there is no risk of water damage as no liquid should come into contact with the wall.

WHEN TO DO: ANY TIME, THOUGH PLANT FROM EARLY SPRING TO EARLY AUTUMN

You will need
* Plastic guttering with end caps
* A paintbrush and exterior gloss paint (optional)
* A saw
* A household drill with 3mm drill bit
* Multipurpose compost
* Water-retaining gel
* Seeds of lettuce, basil, coriander, spinach, chard, rocket, leaf beet, radishes, peas, sunflowers or salad onions
* Brackets, screws and rawl plugs to attach the guttering to the wall

How to do it
You can paint your guttering if you want it to blend with the wall – if so, use an exterior gloss paint and make sure you only paint the outside, as you don't want it to come into contact with the compost. Cut your guttering into the lengths you require, then drill holes in the base, about 10cm apart, to allow for drainage, and attach the end caps.

Fill the guttering with compost mixed with the water-retaining gel, to cut down on future watering. Sow your seeds about 1cm apart and water well. Attach the guttering brackets to the wall using screws, rawl plugs and your drill, then hang up the guttering. Keep well watered. Cut leaves when salad and herb seedlings are about 10cm high, onions when they have formed a bulb. For harvesting pea and sunflower shoots, see p. 39.

STEAL THEIR STYLE: MAKE A HANGING BOTTLE HERB GARDEN

This is a great way to turn plastic bottles into a hanging garden with laid-back charm. Herbs and salad leaves will grow happily in these old bottles strung from balcony railings and they look fantastic if you paint them bright colours.

WHEN TO DO: EARLY SPRING – MID-SUMMER

You will need

* 4 large plastic bottles, such as 1-litre mineral-water bottles or milk containers
* Scissors
* Colourful exterior gloss paint
* A paintbrush
* A nail or spike such as a bradrawl to pierce holes in the bottles' bottoms
* A hole punch
* Horticultural grit
* Multipurpose compost
* 4 herb plants, such as parsley, coriander, tarragon, thyme, oregano, chives or basil
* Strong string

How to do it

Cut off the bottom half of each bottle using scissors. Paint the outside of the bottles with exterior gloss paint. Once it is dry, pierce several holes in the base, making sure they are at least 3mm in diameter. With the hole-punch make two holes at the top of each container through which you'll tie the string and hang it.

Place a layer of grit at the bottom of each bottle. Mix the compost with more grit (at a ratio of about four to one) and half-fill the bottle planters with it. The added grit makes the

compost drain really well; this is essential for herbs as they hate their roots to be waterlogged. Position the herb plants in the compost and firm them in, filling the bottles with more compost. Water well. Thread the string through the holes and hang up your herb garden somewhere sunny and where you can reach the plants for easy pickings.

Easy tip

Don't throw away the top halves of the bottles; push them, neck down, into compost next to big, thirsty plants such as tomatoes, courgettes and potted fruit trees. When you water, fill up the bottle and you can be sure the water will get right down to the roots of the plant rather than evaporating from the surface of the compost on a hot day.

Inspiration

Mike's Manhattan fire escape

If you find yourself constantly complaining about how little space you have on your balcony, just think: 'What would Mike do?' Thirty-year-old New Yorker Mike Lieberman gardens on a 90cm by 60cm fire escape outside his fourth-floor apartment in Manhattan. A self-professed 'Brooklynite' with zero experience in gardening or farming, Mike just shows what can be done with a bit of creativity and determination.

Every centimetre of space is covered with recycled food and drink containers, whether hanging from the railings or crammed on the iron floor. You'd never know these colourful pots, painted with a milk-based, eco-friendly paint, started life as containers for mayonnaise or ice cream. He also uses old coffee containers and upturned fizzy-drink bottles, cut in half, as hanging containers, which are strung from the railings and painted with colourful patterns. The effect is eclectic, eccentric and totally charming, especially when salad leaves, kales, brightly coloured rainbow chard and blood-veined sorrel are tumbling over the sides.

Project
ON YOUR BIKE: MAKE A TYRE PLANTER

Tyres make great planters because they retain moisture and absorb warmth from the sun, so they're ideal for thirsty, heat-loving plants such as courgettes, squashes, chillies and tomatoes. They can be stacked as high or low as you like: a low stack is perfect for salads and annual herbs such as coriander and basil; add a few more tyres and you have root space for strawberries; another couple more and you could get a bumper crop of tumbling tomatoes, salad potatoes or French beans.

Use any discarded bicycle tyres – either those you have lying around or ones you can pick up from bike repair shops which will be glad to see the back of them. They chuck out dozens of tyres every day and will be only too happy to let you take some off their hands. Use the thickest ones you can find, though – you'll need far fewer mountain bike tyres to make a decent pot than those sleek racing-bike versions. If you have lots of space use adult tyres, but if not, ask for children's tyres or those from folding bikes.

WHEN TO DO: ANY TIME, THOUGH PLANT UP FROM MID-SPRING TO MID-AUTUMN
You will need
* At least 5 old bicycle tyres
* Plastic cable ties
* 1 black plastic rubble sack
* Broken crocks or polystyrene pieces
* Scissors or belt hole puncher
* Multipurpose compost
* Plants of your choice (see above)

How to do it
Stack one tyre on top of another, then tie them together with cable ties, carefully puncturing the rubber with scissors or a belt hole puncher. Repeat until you have a stack.

Push the rubble sack into the centre of the stack to line the planter, making decent-sized drainage holes in the base of it so that water can escape. To plant, first put a layer of broken crocks or polystyrene on the bottom, then fill up with compost and get planting. Water well and place in a sunny, sheltered spot.

Tyre planters are perfect for heat-loving plants such as sweet potatoes and basil

The City Farmer's Balcony

In the old days, you knew where you were: the countryside was for farms, the city was for shops and office blocks. If a city had a green space, it was designed purely for rest and relaxation – an oasis in the smoke – whether London's royal parks ('the lungs of the city'), Paris's Jardin du Luxembourg or Manhattan's Central Park. The last thing you'd expect to come across in an urban centre was a vegetable garden. Broccoli, lettuce and tomatoes came wrapped in cellophane, not growing among the high-rises.

Beekeeping on the roof of the Palais Garnier opera house in Paris

Beekeeping on the roof of the Palais Garnier opera house in Paris

But these days, fruit and vegetable growing has never been more popular, even in the heart of cities. Now it's chic to eulogise over the superior sweetness of just-dug carrots and trendy to know your heritage tomatoes. Every day, more balconies are commandeered by newly enthused gardeners, inspired by the benefits of growing their own fruit and vegetables – even if it's just a few herbs or some delectable sun-warmed tomatoes. Sitting in a deck chair, picking a perfectly ripe strawberry while looking out over a city skyline is not a bad idea of bliss.

Some people aren't content merely to cultivate their own little piece of paradise in the sky, though; they are realising the potential all around them on a much larger scale. Think of all those many hectares of untapped flat-roof space on the top of office blocks, apartment blocks and warehouses. In London alone there are 100 square kilometres of flat-roof space that could grow food. A new breed of growers is intent on turning these roofs into sky farms to produce fresh fruit and vegetables for local residents, restaurants or office workers.

Concerned about the sustainability of global farming, their aim is to grow food but also to look at cities in a new way: improving our cityscape planning so we incorporate greener, more productive spaces in the future.

Not only are these people growing fresh fruit and vegetables, but they're also conserving rainwater, making compost, farming worms and keeping bees. In Manhattan, warehouse roofs have become sky farms; in Vancouver and Chicago, restaurant roofs have been turned into verdant market gardens for the freshest food for the table. In east London, there are even plans to transform the roof of a vacant multi-storey car park into a vegetable garden using half-tonne builder's bags of soil – there are no worries about load-bearing with a structure built for cars. In St Petersburg, Russia, residents fed up with having to travel miles to find green space are planting up the roofs of their vast concrete tower blocks with crops and sharing the proceeds.

Young, environmentally aware and decidedly urban, these city farmers are leading a food-growing revolution that more of us are joining every day. However small your own little bit of sky, these people offer inspiration for creating an edible, more sustainable oasis high above the traffic. And why just stop at food when you can be farming worms or keeping bees too? The urban buzz is truly just beginning.

City farmers: young, environmentally aware and decidedly urban

Growing food in cities – why it matters

Setting up fruit and vegetable farms on city rooftops is not just a fun idea – a vanity project for privileged eco worriers – it also makes sound sense. To understand why one has to look at global food production and the trends for the future. Many experts now believe that we cannot rely on traditional farming to provide all our food in years to come; global agricultural land is shrinking year by year, while the population continues to grow. On top of that, dwindling oil supplies threaten traditional farming methods that are reliant on fuel to cultivate their acres, fertilise their crops and transport produce thousands of miles across the world. Intensive farming methods have also led to widespread mismanagement of the soil structure, so the topsoil is washed away, its fertility needing to be replenished artificially with oil-industry-derived fertilisers. And so the cycle continues.

Throw global warming into the mix – with increasingly unpredictable global weather patterns of drought and flood – and it's no wonder we're less confident of our future food supply than ever before. Until the scientists can find alternative energy sources that meet our requirements, oil is going to become more expensive and food prices are likely to rise, too. Of course, a few pots of carrots are not going to make us self-sufficient, but little steps... Planting up roofs and balconies has another environmental benefit: keeping the buildings cool in summer, reducing the damaging 'urban heat island effect' and cutting down on the use of energy-guzzling air conditioning.

Conversely, in parts of the world that experience low temperatures, planting up roofs keeps the heat within buildings. Planted roofs and balconies also hold rainwater, even if temporarily, thus reducing pressure on city storm drains which can otherwise flood, forcing sewage and other pollutants into rivers and the sea. Not a bad roll call of benefits for simply planting a few fruit and vegetables.

We are at the beginning of a revolution in the way we see our cities; we are no longer content to watch empty spaces go unused while we fly in expensive, unsustainably grown crops from distant countries. People want to know where their food has come from and how it was grown. And what better way to know that than to grow it yourself?

Be a city farmer

Of course, we don't all have a handy empty warehouse or communal apartment-block roof above our heads that is capable of carrying a 15cm layer of soil, nor do we share the inclination to do something so ambitious, but there are elements of big projects like this that are worth applying even to a small balcony or roof terrace. You can still set up a surprisingly impressive urban allotment in the sky, not only bringing plenty of delicious fresh food to the table, but also creating a more sustainable environment, saving rainwater, making compost, or even keeping your own bees.

When it comes to choosing crops, budding rooftop city farmers might want to concentrate on those that are particularly productive, such as kale, new potatoes and tomatoes, and on those you can grow in succession for a rolling supply. You'll also want to make the best use of every possible centimetre of growing space you have – by interplanting, underplanting and other cunning ways in which you can cram as many crops in as possible. When it comes to containers, bigger is better – If you have the space, and weight restrictions allow, why not even try raised beds?

A ROOFTOP FARM OVERLOOKING MANHATTAN

Not many farms have a perfect view of the Empire State Building, but then Eagle Street is no ordinary farm. A 560-square-metre organic vegetable farm in Brooklyn, New York, it's located on the roof of a disused bagel factory. Rows of spinach, carrots, tomatoes and peppers bask in the sun, growing in a 10–15cm layer of soil, overlooking the skyscrapers. Strutting chickens and beehives complete the idyllic scene. On Sundays a market is held downstairs where people can buy all the fresh crops grown above their heads – other harvests end up in the kitchens of nearby restaurants.

Eagle Street Rooftop Farm was set up not only to grow vegetables for local people but also to raise awareness of how food is produced. Co-founder Annie Novak is passionate about urban green spaces, city flora and fauna and self-sufficiency. 'If putting food on a rooftop revolutionises the way we think about our health, the effect agriculture has on our ecosystem and where our food comes from, then I'm happy to grow it up against the skyline', she says.

It's not just awareness-raising and fresh radishes that make Eagle Street Rooftop Farm an exciting addition to the city. Storm-water runoff is a big problem for New York's drain network, and the more roofs are planted up with crops like this one, the more pressure can be reduced on the city's overtaxed sewage system.

Sustainability is key for this sort of enterprise, and at Eagle Street as much water is reused as possible. Rainwater is collected for irrigating the crops and no overhead sprayers are used because the wind would blow much of the water away. Instead, watering is done by drip lines or by hand and any crops are washed over a bin so the water can be reused on the seedlings.

How to make your crops work hard so you don't have to

A city farmer's balcony is all about growing as much food as possible in a small space. Follow these tips and you'll keep your mini city farm in good shape.

Quick crops for an extra harvest

Fast-growing plants such as radishes, cut-and-come-again salad leaves and peas for pea shoots are great to sow around the edge of pots containing larger, slower-growing crops such as courgettes, beans or strawberries. They don't take up much space or nutrients and you can be eating them within the month, leaving space for the main plant to grow into as it matures. As an added benefit, these crops shade the compost, reducing water evaporation on hot days.

High and low

Underplant tall plants with lower, more shade-tolerant ones. Try the '3 Sisters' pot (right) for a clever combination. Tall plants such as runner beans will grow up a wigwam in the centre, which leaves space around the edge for compact plants like rocket or parsley, or those that trail over the sides, such as strawberries or tumbling tomatoes. Also use any nearby vertical supports, so you may have peas or beans at the back of a container with lower, bushy plants such as courgettes in the front.

Always have plants waiting in the wings

Rather than sowing a new crop once the previous one has been harvested, why not sow a batch in advance in small pots? This way you will always stay one step ahead and have little plants ready to pop in the minute the pot is free.

In winter and early spring, sow seeds inside on a sunny windowsill; otherwise sow in small pots in a sheltered spot outside once all risk of frost is past. When replacing a crop, dig up the old plants, shaking off as much compost as you can, then top up with trowelfuls of fresh potting compost, garden compost or wormery casts to replenish the fertility before planting.

A eulogy to sweetcorn

Homegrown sweetcorn thrown into boiling water within minutes of picking and eaten with plenty of butter is one of the most sublime treats the edible gardener can experience. It's delectably sweet since the sugar has not had time to turn to starch, as it does in shop-bought versions, and super-crisp too. However, you will need a sheltered site because wind can flatten a crop to the ground.

The 'supersweet' or 'tendersweet' varieties are the most delicious – particularly 'Sweet Nugget' and 'Mirai', which has 15cm-long cobs that are perfect for children.

If growing from seed, start sweetcorn off in 9cm pots in mid-spring on a sunny windowsill, sowing one seed per pot about 2cm deep and then transplanting in late spring/early summer. Alternatively, sow direct outside in late spring into the pots you're planning to grow it in. Sweetcorn is wind-pollinated, so plant it in blocks rather than rows to enable the pollen on the tassels to reach other plants. Aim for a maximum of three plants in a 30cm pot (several pots are best to ensure good pollination).

Keep well watered and feed every fortnight with a high-potash feed such as tomato food or liquid seaweed. To test when the cobs are ready to pick, push your fingernail into one of the kernels – if the liquid is milky, they're ready, if it's clear, put the saucepan away for a few more days.

Project
PLANT A '3 SISTERS' POT

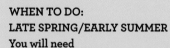

This combination of three crops in one pot was traditionally grown by Native Americans and rather sweetly takes its name from the fact that the plants look after each other. Sweetcorn provides something for the beans to climb up, while they in turn add nitrogen to the soil. This benefits the sweetcorn and squash and the latter helpfully shades the roots of the other plants, protecting them from the drying effects of the sun. If you can't find a compact squash, use a climbing variety, but make sure you can provide something for it to climb up nearby or it will soon rampage out of the pot and over the floor.

WHEN TO DO:
LATE SPRING/EARLY SUMMER
You will need
✳ A large, lightweight pot such as a plastic tub, about 60cm in diameter
✳ Multipurpose compost
✳ 1 compact squash (such as 'Sunburst') or courgette (such as 'Tuscany')
✳ 5 sweetcorn seedlings
✳ 10 climbing bean seedlings

How to do it
Fill the pot with compost, then plant the squash in the centre and space the sweetcorn seedlings out evenly. Plant two bean seedlings at the base of each sweetcorn and water well.

Encourage the beans to climb up the sweetcorn by winding their tops around them as they grow. Place in a sunny, sheltered spot, keep well watered and feed every fortnight with a liquid seaweed feed once the squash starts to form fruits.

10 city farmer crops that just keep on coming

Keep yourself in the following crops all summer long by sowing these every couple of weeks from spring right through to late summer. A 'conveyor belt' of around four medium–large containers (at least 30cm in diameter) at different stages of growth should provide you with a rolling supply of each of the following crops. If you're growing in an average-sized raised bed, sow a row every two weeks instead.

Beetroot

Baby beets roasted in the oven and served with feta and new potatoes are one of the pleasures of early summer. If you sow them successionally you can harvest them small when they are really tender and sweet. Sliced paper-thin, they are also wonderful raw. Don't forget you can eat the leaves, too – delicious in salads or steamed – so this works as a rolling salad crop as well.

Sow seeds about 4cm apart direct into medium–large containers placed in a sunny spot. Do this every two weeks from mid-spring to mid-summer. Harvest when the beets are the size of ping-pong balls. Good varieties include the mini-sized 'Pablo' and 'Pronto', 'Boltardy', 'Bull's Blood' (its purple leaves are particularly good in salads) and 'Chioggia', which has striking concentric rings when you cut it in half.

Carrots

See p. 48.

Salad onions

These are so useful in the kitchen – whether in stir-fries, salads or scattered over the top of soups – and take up very little room. Once sown – 1cm deep, 3cm apart – they need no attention. Harvest by pulling them up when required.

Chard

(to eat raw in salads as a baby leaf)
See p. 39.

French beans

See p. 34.

Lettuce

See p. 36.

Spinach

See p. 39.

Rocket

See p. 39.

Radishes

See p. 39.

Sugarsnap & mange tout peas

Regular podding peas are not ideal for growing in small spaces such as balconies because you don't get left with an awful lot of actual pea once you have shelled them. Sugarsnap and mange tout varieties, however, are much more rewarding in containers as you can eat the whole pod. They're also so delectably sweet straight after picking that you'll be tempted to eat them raw rather than steam them or stir-fry with garlic and ginger – also delicious.

Grow them in medium–large pots or deep window boxes, providing twiggy sticks, netting or multiple lengths of rough garden twine for them to climb up. (These peas climb via tendrils, so they aren't good at clinging to smooth surfaces such as bamboo canes.) Or try planting them in hanging baskets where the peas will hang down rather than climb up. Good varieties of sugarsnaps include the relatively dwarf-growing 'Cascadia', 'Sugar Rae', 'Sugar Bon' and 'Zuccola', while 'Sugar Snap' will grow fairly tall. Dwarf 'Sweet Green' and 'Norli' are good dwarf mange touts.

Sow seeds in pots or direct into the ground outside from mid-spring until early autumn, 5cm deep and 5cm apart, in a sunny spot. Keep well watered. (For growing pea tips for salads, see p. 39.)

Inspiration
A SANCTUARY IN THE SMOKE

The screeching rabbit run of traffic that is north London is only metres away, but you wouldn't know it standing on this delightful little roof garden, tucked away in a side street. Overlooked by grimy windows and the unloved rear ends of city housing, this charming spot belongs to Acorn House, a restaurant set up by the Shoreditch Trust, a charity that works to alleviate poverty in east London through regeneration. The roof garden has been created to show the restaurant's commitment to sustainability as well as to show local trainee chefs the link between 'field' and fork, but it also works as an inspiration for anyone who wants to transform a bit of dusty asphalt into a peaceful oasis.

Deep planters line the edges of the roof, made from tough plastic sacks faced with timber. At the end of a shady bamboo tunnel of runner beans, dotted with scarlet flowers, a fan-trained apple tree basks against a warm brick wall. Blackberries weave their way along a bamboo screen, while handsome-leaved summer squashes jostle for space with bionic-looking tomato bushes, their fruits still green but prolific. There are sweetcorn, globe artichokes, pink-flowered strawberries and a pot overflowing with lemon verbena. It's no wonder Acorn House's sous-chef John (see p. 93) likes to escape up here whenever he can, watering, weeding or just having a breather from the kitchen heat. 'It's lovely up here; there's lots of bees,' he enthuses, dashing from crop to crop and imagining what he can do with it in the kitchen.

The pumpkins might end up in ravioli with walnuts, the tomatoes in a green salsa or side salad, while the lemon verbena is destined for sorbets, ice creams, even a Béarnaise sauce. Runner beans and courgettes would make a fine risotto, he decides, and the blackberries could be mashed into a wild berry Eton mess. While he's the first to admit this little garden couldn't feed his customers regularly, it undeniably makes a delicious contribution.

10 city farmer troopers – crops that give a lot back

Some crops you shower with attention and they reward you with a measly few fruits – aubergines can be a prime example; others demand very little from you but give you a seemingly endless supply of leaves or fruit in return. These are the troopers of the vegetable world, perfect for those trying to create an allotment on high as they will make a real impression on your table. You never know, you may even find yourself self-sufficient in some of them.

Broad beans

Not only are broad beans a delicious early crop, maturing at the start of summer, they are also one of the prettiest vegetable plants you can grow, with delightful, black and white flowers that rival the sweet pea for fragrance. As long as you choose a dwarf variety, such as 'Sutton', there's no reason why you can't grow these beans in pots.

Sow seeds in the autumn in a raised bed, pot or grow bag, 5cm deep and about 15cm apart. You can also sow them in early spring. When the plants start looking floppy, prop them with twiggy sticks or canes and string. Don't pick the pods until they're about 15cm long, then look forward to a long feast of beans – they are wonderful steamed, then popped out of their skins, in warm salads with feta cheese and the first potatoes and beetroot of the year. You can also eat the tops which, when lightly steamed, taste rather like spinach. A harbinger of the new season.

Runner beans

A wigwam of runner beans garlanded with pink or red blossom, buzzing with bees and with long flat pods of beans rivals any ornamental flower in the prettiness stakes. They are also the most accommodating plants, churning out bean after bean from the moment they get into their stride in mid-summer right up to mid-autumn. You can make the most of their jungly, heart-shaped leaves and romping habit on a balcony by letting them scramble up railings or trellising. Or why not make a flavoursome tunnel of beans, see p. 92.

Sow runner beans about 5cm deep and 5cm apart in early summer directly into the container you're growing them in – a raised bed, grow bag or pot at least 30cm in diameter. Either grow them up a wigwam or position the pot near to a structure the beans can climb up. When the

plants reach the top of the support, pinch out the tops to encourage them to put out side-shoots. Runner beans are happy in full sun but they will also produce a decent crop in the shade. Keep picking the beans and the plant will keep producing more.

Good varieties include the old favourite 'Painted Lady', with its pretty, red and white flowers, 'Scarlet Emperor', 'Enorma' and 'Red Rum'. There are also dwarf varieties such as 'Hestia', although you get many more beans if you grow a climbing variety. Keep the plants well watered and feed them every fortnight with a high-potash feed such as liquid seaweed once the pods start to form.

Tomatoes

See p. 30.

Project

MAKE A RUNNER BEAN TUNNEL

Growing crops up archways, tunnels and pergolas is not only a great way to make the most of limited space, but also creates an atmospheric focal point and some lovely dappled shade to sit in. As this demonstrates, it doesn't have to be a permanent, heavy structure either. Climbing French beans, squashes and cucumbers would also grow happily up bamboo canes such as these.

WHEN TO DO:
MID-SPRING TO EARLY SUMMER
You will need

❋ 2 deep trough-style planters, each at least 1m long
❋ 11 bamboo canes, each at least 2m long
❋ Runner bean seeds (see p. 91)
❋ Strong garden twine
❋ Multipurpose compost
❋ A chair or stepladder to stand on

How to do it

Fill the planters with multipurpose compost and site them about 2m apart. Firmly push five canes, evenly spaced, into the compost in one planter, then repeat with the other. Standing on a chair or ladder, tie the tops of opposite canes together so you have five pairs. Then lay the final cane along the top, tying it in tightly to each of the pairs so that you have a reasonably firm structure. Sow the beans at the foot of the canes – for sowing and growing instructions, see p. 91.

pepper or douse them in cheese sauce and put them under the grill until bubbling. Cook the stems for longer – some people think they rival asparagus when dipped in melted butter – or chop them up and add to risottos for interesting colour and texture. Sow in small pots inside in mid-spring and then transplant to a sunny spot in a raised bed, pot or window box in late spring, planting them about 20cm apart.

New potatoes
See p. 33.

Chillies
See p. 50.

Garlic

It's surprisingly easy to grow a lot of garlic; even on a small balcony you could have a few pots growing merrily away, each one providing you with a good ten plump heads that you can hang up to dry in your kitchen and which will keep for months. A long-storing variety such as 'Solent Wight' is harvested in mid-summer and will keep until the following summer. Another good long-storing variety is the classic garlic of the south of France, the white, bumpy 'Albigensian Wight', while luscious 'wet' garlic 'Early Wight' or 'Purple Wight' are ready in late spring and have a delicious fresh flavour. Don't be tempted to plant supermarket garlic, as it may not be a variety suitable for your climate. Better to buy heads specifically for growing from a garden centre or specialist supplier.

Plant garlic in spring or autumn, breaking the heads into individual cloves and popping them into compost about 15cm apart in raised beds, pots or window boxes, pointy end up so that the tip is just below the surface. Keep them well watered and harvest them when the leaves begin to turn yellow. Have an experimental dig around before you pull up the whole crop, leaves and all.

Courgettes
See p. 49.

Chard

When grown to maturity, chard is one of the most productive vegetables you can grow; pick the outer leaves and the plant will keep going for up to nine months. The bonus of chard is that if you grow 'Bright Lights' or 'Rainbow' chard, with its vivid stems of yellow, purple and pink, the plant is a lovely sight too. 'Swiss' chard has relatively tame, white stems but perhaps a finer taste; steam the leaves as you would spinach and add plenty of butter and black

You can eat garlic fresh, but if you want to store it, hang it up somewhere warm and dry for about three weeks until the leaves turn papery, then roughly plait them together and hang them up in the kitchen next to the cooker.

Kale

This earthy brassica is a real performer and you'll be picking the leaves from late summer right through to late spring. Kale is delicious in soups, as a side vegetable, or even stir-fried until crispy and scattered with pumpkin seeds and Parmesan. The only pest you'll be looking out for with this crop will be pigeons, which can strip the plants, but use netting only as a last resort because birds can get caught in it.

Try 'Black Tuscan' kale with its plume of dark, crêpy leaves, or 'Red Russian' with red midribs and such a mild crunch you can eat the small leaves raw in salads. 'Redbor' has frilly leaves and an eye-catching deep burgundy colour.

Sow kale seeds in small pots in late spring and then transfer the seedlings to raised beds, pots or window boxes in mid-summer, planting them about 20cm apart. Firm the plants in well – the test is to pull a leaf; if it breaks before you uproot the plant, it's planted firmly enough.

Raspberries

This fruit bush needs a big pot (about 45cm diameter), but if you can provide this, a few raspberry canes are well worth including on a city farmer's balcony. You'll be amazed how many berries even a few canes produce, and they are so velvety-soft and sweet when picked at the peak of ripeness. Throw them on the top of a meringue, add them to muesli or just eat them right there by the plant.

Plant canes in the autumn, ideally in a John Innes No. 3 compost (if not, a multi-purpose will do), as these plants will be in the pot for several years and so they need a compost that releases nutrients slowly. After planting, mulch the compost with shingle, grit or some other suitable material, because raspberries have shallow roots and might dry out otherwise.

It's best to choose autumn-fruiting varieties for pot growing, such as 'Autumn Bliss', 'Joan J' or yellow 'Fallgold'. Feed the plants every fortnight with a high-potash feed such as liquid seaweed once the berries have started to form. Harvest the fruits from late summer right through to mid-autumn. In late winter, cut all the canes right down to the level of the compost and mulch with fresh garden compost or, if you have it, wormery compost.

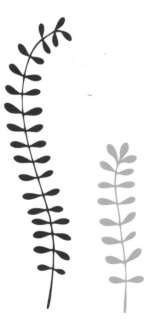

Other city farmer crops

While perhaps not quite as prolifically productive as the previous list, the following crops are all well worth growing since the rewards, when they come, are a real treat.

Sweet peppers

These are surprisingly hot-blooded plants that need the sunniest, most sheltered spot you have going if the fruits are to ripen through to yellow and red, so in some ways they should be treated as exotics. It's not unusual in a less-than-Mediterranean climate for a plant to produce only two or three peppers that are still resolutely green by autumn.

Sow seeds as you would for tomatoes (see p. 30) in early spring inside on a sunny windowsill, transplanting them to pots, raised beds, large window boxes or grow bags (three to a bag) outside only at the beginning of summer. Keep the plants well watered and feed them weekly

with a fertiliser such as liquid seaweed once the fruits have formed. The plants can get quite lanky, so prop them up with canes or tie in to supports if necessary.

Good varieties for containers include 'Redskin' and 'Antohi Romanian'.

Aubergines

Aubergines make wonderfully exotic-looking plants for raised beds or pots, with improbably sensual, violet flowers, furry leaves and, of course, smooth, purple fruits that hang from the stems like dark, glossy treasure. In cool climates, however, they are not easy to get to ripen successfully, so opt for a dwarf mini variety such as 'Orlando', 'Mini Finger', 'Ophelia' or 'Mini Bambino' for the best results. Those gardening in warmer climates might want to choose from luscious 'Moneymaker', 'Black Beauty' or 'Rosa Bianca', with its delicate pink and white skin.

Sow ½cm deep in early spring inside in small pots and then transplant outside to large pots or grow bags (two to each bag) in late spring/early summer and place in a sunny spot. Alternatively, buy plants in late spring and plant them straight out. Feed once the fruit is golf-ball-sized with a high-potash feed such as liquid seaweed. Harvest mini varieties when the fruits are 5–10cm long. Aubergines are delicious cooked in ratatouille or barbecued on skewers with chunks of halloumi cheese and courgette.

Cucumbers

Denser and more flavoursome than the watery, shop-bought versions, homegrown cucumbers are really worth the effort. Mini varieties such as 'La Diva' or 'Vega' are particularly good for containers, picked when they are only about 10cm long and sliced lengthways to add to refreshing drinks such as Pimm's, or to homemade tzatziki or Greek salads.

Buy plants in late spring or sow seeds in mid-spring in 9cm pots inside and transplant outside to containers at least 30cm in diameter or grow bags when all risk of frost is past.

Pinch out the growing tip when the plant has five leaves, to encourage it to bush out, and then tie in shoots to a wigwam, trellis or other support. Feed the plants, which look rather like a more delicate climbing courgette, every fortnight with liquid seaweed or any other high-potash feed.

Home-grown cucumbers: denser and more flavoursome than shop-bought versions

Inspiration
WINDY BUT WONDERFUL
– AN EDIBLE OFFICE ROOF

The London skyline stretches out to the horizon, while below Regent's Canal lies straight as a ruler and, from nearby King's Cross station, Eurostar trains are speeding off to Paris. Geese fly by beside kale, chard and cabbages growing in pretty, woven-willow planters on four raised beds. Strawberries nestle under the snow, while the already-plump buds of gooseberries and blackcurrants point to a good growing season ahead. By summer, the rooftop is alive with tomatoes, courgettes, salad and French beans. Feathery carrot tops peek out above the rim of a willow planter, while scratch the surface of the compost and you uncover the white treasure of 'Anya' potatoes. You'd never believe you were on top of a busy international brand consultancy, unless you saw the workers grazing the beds while taking a break, or helping out by planting a few seedlings.

Everywhere there are signs of sustainability on high. Four water butts store water gathered from a small, sloping roof – providing around 30 per cent of the roof garden's watering needs – and a wormery and compost bin process kitchen scraps and prunings which will eventually end up back in the soil as nutritious compost to feed future crops. The latter themselves end up in the staff restaurant downstairs. And so the cycle continues.

The crops clearly love the lavish sunshine the rooftop provides. However, careful measures have been taken to reduce the damaging effects of the frequent wind, so strong that garden furniture is chained to the railings to prevent it skittering across the roof. However, local regulations at this site do not allow windbreaks to be fixed to the railings, so the garden's creators have had to improvise. The soil level in the planters is not only kept fairly low to give

the crops the additional protection of the walls of the containers themselves, but the raised beds are edged in low, woven fencing. The surface of the compost is mulched with a thick layer of cocoa shells to protect against the drying effects of the wind.

As well as this, the choice of crops has been made with the wind very much in mind. Dwarf runner and French beans are happy here but there are no climbing varieties since these would soon be turned to ribbons. Low-lying strawberries, salads and potatoes do well, while the sturdy raspberry canes and redcurrant bushes seem to shrug off the wind, gleaming with juicy, red berries. Rosemary and thyme are similarly unbothered, but there's an absence of tall, lanky crops. Sweetcorn would last only minutes up here.

TOP CROPS FOR A WINDY BALCONY

* Herbs: bay, rosemary, thyme, sage, oregano, chives, parsley
* Radishes
* Rocket
* Lettuce
* Dwarf French and runner beans
* Leeks
* Carrots
* Salad onions
* Chard
* Pak choi
* Kale
* Strawberries
* Blueberries
* Goji berries
* Garlic
* Olives
* Redcurrants
* Gooseberries
* Raspberries
* Potatoes

Project

STEAL THEIR STYLE: HOW TO COPE WITH A WINDY SITE

Balconies and roofs can be notoriously exposed and windy, thanks to a combination of lack of shelter and the funnelling of wind through chicanes of tall buildings. This is a potential problem for the gardener since wind can not only damage and stunt plants, but also quickly dries out the surface of the compost. Windbreaks of woven material such as bamboo, reed or willow screens are often more effective than solid barriers since they filter the wind rather than push it up and over the other side in a turbulent gust. Well-placed evergreen shrubs, such as box, rosemary, elaeagnus or grasses, or a trellis planted with climbing plants can also offer valuable protection.

If planting in raised beds, an additional low fence of woven willow or other screening around the edge will protect the crops within. If planting in pots, try keeping the level of compost fairly low to allow the pot sides to offer some protection and mulch all your pots or raised beds regularly with garden compost, cocoa shells or an organic product such as Strulch Garden Mulch to keep moisture from evaporating from the surface.

you to position the loads over certain points or tell you that the roof needs strengthening.

It's fairly easy to nail together a raised bed using scaffolding boards or other planks, but, for ease, one of the many raised-bed kits available is a good choice. These are basically bottomless square or rectangular frames that can simply be laid down on the floor surface. Those made of plastic, such as Link-a-Bord, are ideal as they are lightweight and can be constructed in minutes without tools. They are also modular, so you can easily add a level to make them deeper, if weight allows, and you can buy additional insect mesh or fleece kits if you want to protect your crops from butterflies and the cold.

Before setting up your raised bed, check that your floor is well waterproofed and that it has a slight fall. All properly designed roofs and balconies, even 'flat' ones, have a slight slope to allow rainwater to drain away. Make sure this path isn't blocked so that water can run away freely. To increase the drainage properties of your raised bed even further, it's a good idea to buy some wire-mesh panels (available from DIY centres) and pop them down on the floor under your raised bed. This raises the level of the compost a little, so allowing water to drain away more easily. On top of the mesh, lay a porous woven membrane such as landscape fabric or weed-suppressing membrane (mini raised-bed kits may come with this already). This membrane will prevent compost from falling into the mesh and onto the roof surface, keeping the floor clean and protecting the roof.

Project

STEAL THEIR STYLE: GROW CROPS IN A SHALLOW RAISED BED

For those with medium to large balconies or roof terraces, a shallow raised bed around a metre square and 15cm deep is a great way really to maximise the crops you can grow in your sky allotment. For those with small balconies there are also plenty of 'mini raised beds' you can buy, which are generally lightweight, flexible bag planters that are perfect for getting the most out of a small space (see above, left). Before adding any considerable raised beds, though, do check with a structural engineeras they may advise

Which crops are best for raised beds?

Crops to grow in a 15-cm deep bed:

* Lettuce and other salads
* Strawberries
* Dwarf French beans
* Runner beans
* Climbing French beans
* Round-rooted carrots
* Garlic
* Onions, shallots
* Courgettes
* Tumbling tomatoes
* Oriental greens such as mizuna, mibuna, tatsoi
* Peas
* Radishes
* Spinach
* Basil, chives, coriander, chervil, dill, oregano, mint, thyme
* Edible flowers such as nasturtiums, marigolds, violas

Crops to grow in a 20-cm deep bed:

* Bush and cordon tomatoes
* Broad beans
* Kale
* Cabbage
* Aubergines
* Chard
* Squash
* Pumpkins
* Cucumber
* Florence fennel
* Leeks
* Parsnips
* Sweet peppers
* Chillies
* Turnips
* Melons
* Rosemary, sage, tarragon, parsley

Crops to grow in a 30-cm deep bed:

* Potatoes
* Sweetcorn
* Beetroot
* Carrots
* Rhubarb
* Fruit trees
* Kiwi fruit
* Blackcurrants
* Raspberries
* Red- and whitecurrants
* Gooseberries
* Blueberries
* Bay

Which compost is best for raised beds?

Since weight is likely to be an issue in a balcony garden it's best to avoid loam-based composts as these are heavier. A good-quality multipurpose compost is a fine start, mulched with cocoa shells or Strulch Garden Mulch to retain as much moisture as possible. To maintain the fertility of the compost you will need to feed crops as they grow and add a thick layer of organic matter in the form of garden compost, spent mushroom compost, wormery casts and/or well-rotted manure at least once a year. A good rule of thumb is to add a trowelful of organic matter and dig it into the soil every time you remove a plant.

City farmer crops when water is in short supply

If you are not lucky enough to have an outside tap on your balcony or roof, or access to a convenient indoor one, watering your plants becomes much more of a chore than it would otherwise be. Tramping through your flat with a heavy watering can several times a day is no one's idea of fun. If you are able to install a rainwater butt outside you can fill your watering can from it easily, and buckets and large, shallow containers left outside will also store rainwater when it falls. But if you don't have easy access to water it is probably best to avoid growing thirsty crops such as potatoes, strawberries, tomatoes, aubergines, peppers, cucumbers, figs, courgettes and raspberries, as these will need watering every day in hot weather. The crops below are relatively drought-tolerant when established, though they will still need a good soak when first planted or sown.

The least thirsty edible crops

* Beetroot
* Carrots
* Spinach
* Chard
* Kale
* Salad onions
* Peas
* Garlic
* Olives
* Sweetcorn
* Globe artichokes
* Goji berries
* Edible flowers such as nasturtiums, marigolds and violas
* Cape gooseberries (right)
* Herbs: bay, rosemary, thyme, sage, oregano, lemon verbena, bronze fennel

Top city farmer crops for a shady balcony

Not all balconies are drenched in sunshine for eight hours a day; some are surrounded by tall buildings and are cast in shadè much of the time, while most will have a tricky shady corner. So what can you plant that will be happy in these conditions? Generally speaking, anything that fruits prefers sun, while those that produce edible leaves are more tolerant of shade. Some crops, such as mint and sorrel, even prefer a shady spot. All the crops below will grow successfully in shade.

Top shade-loving crops

* Salad leaves
* Runner beans
* Blackberries (far right)
* Redcurrants
* Blackcurrants
* Gooseberries
* Rocket (below)
* Raspberries
* Tayberry
* Sorrel
* Peas (right)
* Beetroot
* Radishes
* Chard
* Spinach
* Herbs: parsley, coriander
* Morello cherry
* Victoria plum

Fruit trees with a head for heights

Nothing turns a city rooftop into a verdant paradise so much as an orchard of potted fruit trees, especially when they are in blossom, buzzing with pollinating bees, or dripping with fruit. But even if you have a tiny balcony, it's really worth including a fruit tree. Whether it's a single minarette pear tree or a line of fan-trained peaches, apricots, plums and espaliered apples edging a terrace, fruit trees bring a structure and a delicious sense of maturity to a balcony or roof garden.

All year round they offer something – from a beautiful winter silhouette to a froth of spring blossom, leafy shade and shelter for other crops, and then finally they give up their sun-warmed fruits, all the sweeter for having been grown right there.

Which tree to choose?

Fruit trees are happy in pots as long as they are grown on a dwarfing rootstock – any specialist supplier can help you select the right one for your balcony if you are unsure. Either grow a traditional-shaped tree or experiment with some of the lovely trained shapes and grow them up against your wall – they'll really benefit from the warmth the bricks retain from the sun's heat and are often more productive than traditional bush-shaped trees.

The easiest form of fruit tree for even the tiniest of balconies is a minarette (sometimes called a ballerina or upright cordon). These take up hardly any space since they grow as single upright stems, reaching about 1.8m tall, with short, fruit-bearing side branches that need minimal pruning in summer. U-shaped cordons are just as attractive, with a pair of upright stems studded with fruit, while 'double-U' cordons are perhaps the most ornamental of all.

If you have a lot of wall space around your terrace or balcony, fan-trained trees look particularly lovely, spreading out their branches against the wall and soaking up the heat absorbed by the building to produce the most delectable fruit. (Allow about 1.8m of horizontal wall space per tree.) Figs, peaches, apricots, cherries and plums all grow happily as fans. Other fruits such as apples and pears can be pruned as espaliers, with horizontal branches coming off a vertical stem, or even as double-U cordons.

For both fans and espaliers, simply fix parallel wires to the wall to tie the branches to, or use your railings as supports. You can train these trees yourself, but it's much easier to buy them ready-trained. They may be considerably more expensive, but since you can expect your potted tree to provide you with a harvest for many years, it's worth investing a little more at the start.

Always check with suppliers to see if you need more than one tree to ensure good pollination. Some fruit trees, such as cherries, apricots and peaches, are self-fertile, so you will get fruit with only one tree; others, such as apples and pears, need a partner nearby to ensure pollination. If you have room for only one apple or pear tree, a 'family' tree, in which three varieties have been grafted onto one rootstock, is ideal.

The top 10 fruit trees for an orchard balcony

Apples
The quintessential orchard fruit that can be grown as a bush on dwarfing rootstock, or as an espalier, minarette, U-shaped cordon or double U. Delectable dessert varieties include 'Discovery', 'Fiesta' and 'Sunset', all of which will pollinate each other. Or try 'Polka', 'James Grieve', 'Braeburn', 'Worcester Pearmain' or 'Cox'. Good cooking varieties include 'Bramley', 'Newton Wonder' and 'Lord Derby'. Or choose a 'family' tree, perfect for small spaces since it combines three varieties on one tree.

Pears
A ripe pear is a wonderful thing, but since they flower early, their crops can be damaged by late frosts. To be on the safe side, cover the branches with fleece if they're in blossom when a frost is forecast. Pears can be grown as a bush on dwarfing rootstock, or as a cordon, espalier, minarette, U-shaped cordon or double U. Good dessert varieties include 'Beurre Hardy', 'Concorde' and 'Doyenné du Comice'. As with apples, it's also worth looking out for 'family' trees that have had three varieties grafted onto one rootstock.

Cherries
Cherries are self-fertile, so you only ever need one tree to ensure a good crop. If you can keep the birds off, that is; netting may be a necessary defence as the fruit ripens. Expect beautiful blossom and lots of fruit when the tree is established. Grow cherries as a bush on dwarfing rootstock, as a minarette or as a fan against a warm wall. Good varieties include 'Stella' and 'Sunburst'. If you have a shady, north-facing wall, a morello or acid cherry will thrive as a fan, producing tart cherries that are excellent when cooked.

Plums
These accommodating trees deliver heavy crops with very little asked from you in return. Pruning is minimal (and certainly should never be attempted except in summer for fear of fungal infection) and they are self-fertile. The only thing they demand is that the developing fruits are thinned out, otherwise plum trees tend to produce far too many plums one year, followed by nothing the next. Thin plums in mid-summer so they are about 5cm apart. Either grow plums as a bush on dwarfing rootstock or as a fan. 'Victoria' will give a decent crop even in the shade.

Peaches and Apricots
Once you have tasted your first ripe peach or apricot straight from your own tree, there's no going back. Such experiences have to be repeated, and you'll go to no end of trouble to do so. As with all container fruit trees, make sure you buy a tree with the suitable dwarfing rootstock. A good dwarf peach is 'Bonanza', or try 'Champion' or 'Aprigold' for a dwarf apricot. All these can be grown as free-standing trees in pots and need little pruning; alternatively they can be grown as fans.

Both peaches and apricots are hardy when dormant over winter, but since they blossom early in the spring, the flowers are susceptible to frost damage. Bring the tree inside when in blossom if frost is forecast or cover with horticultural fleece if it is trained against a wall. Although self-fertile, both trees can benefit from a bit of help with pollination to ensure you get a good crop – when the flowers are open, dab the pollen gently with a soft brush and rub it onto the surrounding flower. Peach leaf curl is a nasty fungal disease, so if you can find a dwarf variety that claims resistance to this disease, buy it.

Figs
Grow as a fan or a standard form. (See p. 123)

Olives
See p. 122.

Lemons
See p. 124.

Calamondin orange
See p. 124.

How to plant and grow fruit trees

You can grow fruit trees in a pot that is at least 30cm in diameter and 30cm deep. Galvanised dustbins are ideal, look surprisingly elegant and can be picked up from hardware stores cheaply. Other heavier options include halved wooden barrels or terracotta pots, while for super-lightweight versions consider plastic planters or rubber tub trugs. All will need drainage holes drilled into the base if they are not already there, and also should be tied in to some sort of support, as a fruit tree in full leaf can really catch the wind. Since fruit trees will live for many years, it's best to plant them in a soil-based compost which releases nutrients slowly, such as John Innes No. 3. Place the trees in a sunny spot to get a really good, sweet crop.

Feed potted fruit trees every fortnight from blossom time to mid-autumn with a high-potash feed such as liquid seaweed and keep them well watered. It's a good idea to mulch the surface of the compost (with shingle or cocoa shells, for example) to keep moisture in. The traditional time to plant fruit trees is in the dormant season from mid-autumn to early spring, though you can pick up potted trees all year round. The pruning required varies depending on the form and type of fruit tree – it's worth buying from a specialist supplier because they will provide detailed instructions.

Highly sustainable

Your sky-high city farm may be small, but that doesn't mean it can't be sustainable. Whether you're capturing rainwater, turning your kitchen scraps into fertile compost or even keeping bees, you can create your own little eco haven in the sky, a self-sustaining eden that not only puts food on the table but helps the wider environment too.

Be a worm farmer

If you have a balcony, you probably have space for a wormery, and that means you can be turning your carrot peelings and apple cores into lovely food for your growing plants.

Wormeries are carefully designed worm farms in which layers of wriggly, red brandling worms – different from the ones you usually see in garden soil – munch through your kitchen waste and produce both rich compost and nutritious liquid feed that you can dilute (one part worm liquid to 10 parts water) and feed to your plants.

Wormeries take up less space than compost bins, so they are a better choice for balcony gardeners. The waste is also broken down at a much faster rate than in a traditional compost bin and they don't need to be placed on earth, unlike compost bins, since any liquid that collects in them can be drained off with a handy tap and then fed to your plants. Also, again unlike compost bins, wormeries can digest both raw and cooked vegetables, bread, cake, pasta and plenty of other food waste – though not meat and fish scraps – so they will really reduce the weight of your kitchen bin. They'll also cut down on your recycling since worms love a third of their food to be shredded cardboard or paper: the perfect use for all that packaging.

As this worm compost is very rich, all that is needed is a handful or two of it to be mixed in with your regular potting compost when you are planting something. It's wonderful as a mulch, added as a layer about 5cm thick around hungry and thirsty plants. It can also be used to freshen up compost when you're taking out crops and replacing them with new ones.

Store rainwater

By saving rainwater in water butts and using it on your plants you're reducing the pressure not only on your city's storm drains – a real problem for cities such as New York and London – but also on yourself: it's much easier to fill a watering can from a water butt on the balcony than to drag a hose through the house from the bathroom tap.

It is easy to plumb a water butt into your downpipe, and kits are readily available which include fittings to the downpipe. You may need a plumber to help you if your downpipe is metal, but if it's plastic you can cut into it yourself with a hacksaw. Obviously, if you live in an apartment block or don't own your building, you would have to check with your building owner before altering the pipe in any way.

If you're worried about the weight of a water butt on your balcony or terrace, bear in mind that 1 litre of water weighs 1kg.

A hive of activity: keeping bees on your roof

'The pleasure is the fascination with what's going on inside the hive. It's a little miracle in there,' says beekeeper Luke Dixon, who keeps hives on rooftops in Soho, the South Bank, and Bloomsbury, in central London.

Safe and secure, out of the way of predators and within flying distance of acres of flowering parks, balconies and back gardens, a city rooftop has so many advantages for beekeeping that it's odd that more of us urbanites aren't already doing it. And we certainly should because, worldwide, bees are in trouble. According to the International Bee Research Association, half of the honeybee population of Britain and the US has disappeared since the 1940s, mainly as a result of fungal disease, habitat destruction and the invasion of parasites. More recently, colony collapse disorder has added to their problems, decimating the global population still further. In 2008, 35 per cent of Europe's 13.6 million honeybees died from colony collapse disorder; between 2007 and 2008, 35 per cent of US bees were wiped out. This is troubling because, quite apart from the honey they provide, bees are vital to the future of our planet. It's estimated that a third of the food we eat comes from sources pollinated by insects, predominantly bees.

Anything we can do to increase the numbers of honeybees is therefore worthwhile, and recently the world's cities have been stepping up to the challenge. In Paris there are hives on the glass roof of the Grand Palais exhibition hall, just off the Champs-Elysées, on the gilded dome of the nineteenth-century Palais Garnier and the roof of the modern Opéra Bastille. In London, the Royal Festival Hall has hives on the roof, while Fortnum & Mason, the high-end store in the city's West End, boasts bespoke hives with Gothic, Roman, Chinese or Mughal arches. Berlin, Tokyo and Washington also have a thriving beekeeping culture. Until recently, New York City classified bees as venomous insects and keeping bees was punishable with a $2,000 fine, so Manhattan beekeepers were forced to disguise their rooftop hives as air-conditioning units or chimneys and keep their activities secret. The ban has now been lifted, so we can expect to hear Manhattan's rooftops resonating with a low hum over the next few years.

A sweet treat awaits anyone who keeps bees on a city roof; urban honey is generally considered to be far richer and more interesting in flavour than rural honey, because of the rich multiflora that is available in cities – from parks to gardens and balconies. In the countryside, bees may dine solely on oilseed rape, resulting in a blander-flavoured honey. Hayfever sufferers may want to try beekeeping too, as by eating a spoonful of local honey every day you can, it is alleged, introduce local pollens into your system, thereby making your body less allergic to them.

Here's the buzz:

The following basic advice will help you get started if you fancy keeping bees on a roof or balcony.

Space You need enough space for the footprint of the hive (60cm^2) plus room to work around it – unstacking the hive and restacking it on the floor while checking the brood, the queen and the honey. The front of the hive should always face away from your flat or dwelling, and as long as there is at least 30cm of space between the front of the hive and any solid barrier, such as a wall, the bees will have enough space to fly out and up.

Money There are initial set-up costs of about £600 for a hive and bees. You will also need a smoker and protective clothes – either a full bee suit or a hat and veil, though these can easily be found secondhand, and washing-up gloves are just as good as beekeeper gloves. Equipment to process the honey can be borrowed.

Time Beekeeping will take a couple of hours of your time a week per hive during the summer, less during the winter.

Honey Little spare honey will be produced in the first year; then, depending on bees, weather and site, you can expect 50–100 jars a hive per year. Honey is harvested once a year.

Security Tie the hives to railings or other supports with a bungee cord or some other strong rope to prevent them blowing over in the wind.

Diseases These are a major problem nowadays and you have to take great care to keep your bees healthy. Join your local beekeeping society for more information.

Support You should not start beekeeping without doing a course and joining your local beekeepers' association, where you will find lots of help and advice.

Some Like It Hot

One of the most exciting things about balcony and roof gardens is how they can give free rein to your fantasies. Don't want to feel like you live in a grey city where it rains all the time? No problem, just buy some plants that remind you of somewhere hotter – whether it's a tropical beach paradise or a dusty Mediterranean hillside.

The exotic balcony

adding gorgeous, hot-blooded non-edible companions into the mix. For a Mediterranean feel choose oleanders – evergreen shrubs with spiky leaves and plumes of pink, white or purple flowers – geraniums, lavenders, hibiscus or neat box balls. For a more tropical ambience, go for bamboos, tree ferns, succulents such as the spiky and magnificent century plant (*Agave americana*), or palm trees – the Canary Island date palm (*Phoenix canariensis*), the Chusan palm (*Trachycarpus fortunei*) and cycad or king sago palm (*Cycas revoluta*) all thrive in containers on a balcony.

Escapsim is well within your grasp when you're gardening above the ground. As confined microcosms, balconies and roofs seem to cry out for theatrical transformations and it's amazing what effects you can create with just a few plants. It's hard to turn a regular back garden surrounded by featherboarded fencing and a view of your neighbour's washing into something exotic, but a balcony or roof above the city is a blank slate. After all, it's already set apart from the world below, so why not go the whole hog and create a fantasy world – a tropical paradise?

Surround yourself with the scent of orange blossom, cut your own lemons into your G and T. You never know, if you're lucky you might even be able to savour your own olives. Some glamorous plants are surprisingly easy to grow, while others, such as citrus, are a little fussy, but with a bit of attention, an exotic jungle is well within grasp.

Recreate a Mediterranean feel by painting walls white or terracotta. Consider handmade terracotta planters, or glazed deep blue pots. You can also emphasise the escapist theme by

The top 5 crops for the exotic balcony

If you want to give your roof or balcony a hot-blooded flavour, these delectable fruits are a great start.

Olives

The gnarled, twisty trunks and cloud of silvery, pointed leaves of these trees are horticultural shorthand for hot climates, conjuring instant images of dusty Italian hillsides or ancient Greek groves. And yet these trees are surprisingly hardy in cooler climates, too, and can exist happily on urban balconies and roof terraces even in northern Europe, benefiting from the mild microclimate of the city.

Olive trees (*Olea europaea*) are beautiful and elegant – find a style-conscious balcony owner and odds on they'll have an olive tree nestling in a corner somewhere. Wind-resistant and low-maintenance, they will happily stay in the same pot for several years and don't need much pruning. If you're lucky, you might even get an edible crop too (see right).

A two-year-old standard tree is a good choice for a balcony, and is relatively cheap, but go for an older tree is you want instant gnarled maturity. Plant in a sunny, sheltered spot, ideally in a half-and-half mix of a multipurpose compost and John Innes No 3. Prune lightly in mid-spring to maintain shape, or more heavily in early to mid-summer, and feed your tree fortnightly with liquid seaweed from May to September. Repot the tree every third or fourth year in spring, into an only slightly larger pot each time, as olives like their roots to be restricted.

Over winter olive trees are surprisingly hardy; they can tolerate night-time temperatures of -3°C regularly, and even down to minus -7°C now and then. Any lower than that and you should protect the tree with several layers of horticultural fleece and the pot with plastic bubble wrap to prevent the roots from freezing.

Cure your own olives

If you're lucky enough to get a good crop of olives from your tree, why not try turning them from inedible bullets into delicious home-cured olives? The process takes 2 weeks, though, so it is not for the impatient.

When to do: Mid-autumn when the fruits ripen

You will need

* ❋ Olives
* ❋ 1 large container
* ❋ Salt
* ❋ White wine vinegar
* ❋ Garlic, lemon slices or herbs such as oregano or rosemary (optional)
* ❋ Olive oil
* ❋ Airtight containers for storing the olives

How to do it

Rinse the olives in water and drain. Bash the olives on a chopping board with a rolling pin to crack the flesh, leaving the stones in. Place the olives in a large container and cover with fresh water, making sure they are submerged by pressing them down with a plate or similar item. Leave for 24 hours. Drain the olives and cover again with fresh water. Repeat this process for 10–14 days.

Now make the brine: for 1kg of olives, mix 1 litre of water with 100g of salt. Soak for 2 days. Drain and soak in a solution of 80 per cent vinegar to 20 per cent water, adding garlic cloves, slices of lemon or herbs for extra flavour if you wish. Decant into airtight containers and cover with a layer of olive oil so they are completely submerged, then refrigerate for two days. You can now – finally – eat your homegrown olives, though they will store for several months if kept in the fridge.

Figs to fight over

A sprawling, fan-trained fig tree in a pot is a majestic sight; the hand-shaped leaves release a marvellously 'figgy' scent if you brush past them, particularly on hot days. And then there are the impossibly succulent fruits, swelling through the summer until they all but burst open to reveal their sweet, dark flesh. Figs are an ideal choice for pot growing because they prefer to have their roots confined, and they're easy to train into loose fan shapes by tying branches against a warm wall.

To ensure a crop where your climate is cool, protect the baby fruits over winter by tying sleeves of plastic bubble wrap loosely around them – making sure to leave them open-ended so that air can still circulate. Any fruits that are larger than pea-size by autumn should be removed, and pinch out the growing shoots of the tree in early summer so that only five leaves remain per shoot.

'Brown Turkey' is a reliable variety with delicious, purple-fleshed fruits. Other good ones to try are 'Brunswick' and 'Violetta'. Plant in multipurpose compost or John Innes No. 3 in a pot no smaller than 45cm in diameter. Place in a sunny, sheltered spot, keep well watered and feed with liquid seaweed every fortnight throughout the growing season.

For easy citrus,
Calamondin orange
trees are a great
beginner's choice

CITRUS

Citrus trees are a popular choice for the
exotically inclined balcony or rooftop gardener
because they bring a real dash of glamour.
Any urban skyline looks beautiful when seen
through a screen of potted standard lemon or
lime trees. The leaves also give off a wonderfully
zesty lemon scent when rubbed, though this is
nothing compared to the fragrance of their
flowers, which are often produced all year round.
Citrus trees often have flowers and ripe fruit on
them at the same time, but they do need a hot,
sheltered spot for the fruit to ripen.

CALAMONDIN ORANGE MARMALADE

Makes 1 jar
* 150g chopped Calamondin oranges
* 500ml water
* 200g sugar
* A jar

Sterilise the jar; wash in hot, soapy water, rinse
and then place upside down in a cool oven at
140°C/275°F/Gas 1 for at least ½ hour. Wash the
Calamondins, then cut them in half and remove
the pips. Slice them finely, with the rind on, then
put them in a saucepan with the water and boil,
uncovered, for 15 minutes. Remove from the
heat and leave to steep overnight with the lid on.

The next day, add the sugar and bring to a
rolling boil for about half an hour – it's ready
when a spoonful dropped onto a cold plate
cools to a jam-like consistency. Pour into the
sterilised jar.

Which citrus tree should I choose?

For easy pickings:

Calamondin orange is perhaps the best choice for beginner gardeners. These glossy trees constantly produce intensely scented flowers which develop into small, round fruits that are too sour to eat raw but make delicious, tangy marmalade. They can also be cut into segments and added to cool drinks. The biggest benefit of Calamondin oranges (× *Citrofortunella microcarpa*), though, is that this is the only citrus that is happy to be over-wintered in heated living rooms – it can even be grown all year inside.

For cooler, frost-prone climates, the following tough customers are good choices:

Japanese bitter orange is as tough as they come; this citrus can handle short periods of frost unprotected. The plant will stop growing at temperatures below 12°C and will lose its leaves, but it will then put out new shoots in the spring. It is happiest planted near a south-facing wall. Flowers appear in spring and transform the bush into a cloud of scented, white blooms, but beware the long, sharp thorns. The fruits are too bitter to eat raw, but they can be made into a tangy marmalade.

Kumquat is another variety suitable for the inexperienced gardener, which can be over-wintered outside even during brief cold snaps. It makes a very attractive container plant, producing a multitude of small, oval-shaped orange fruits which you eat skin and all. 'Nagami' is a reliable and productive variety.

Lemon 'Meyer's Lemon' is a cross between a lemon and an orange. This delightful compact tree has sweet fruits and pure white star-shaped flowers that appear at the same time. This variety can cope with occasional frosts; any colder than that and it would be best to overwinter it inside (see below).

The following varieties are fabulous, but frost tender:

If you are lucky enough to garden in a frost-free climate, choose from **mandarins, satsumas and clementines, lemons, oranges, limes or grapefruit**. If you live in a cool climate but really want to try growing one of these frost-intolerant citruses, bring the tree inside into a cool bright room that is kept at a temperature between 5–12°C from the second month of autumn to the second month of spring. If this cannot be achieved, put the tree in the coolest, brightest room you have, right by the window, and keep watering to a minimum. Trees may lose their leaves while kept inside in the house, but they should recover the following year, even if they lose their crop.

Growing citrus

Plant trees in a sunny, sheltered spot in a free-draining compost such as John Innes No. 2 with 20 per cent added grit. Citrus plants don't mind being quite snug and a five-year-old tree can be quite happy in a 30cm-diameter pot.

Feed plants with specialist citrus food – there are different types for winter and summer – and water with rainwater rather than tap, if possible. Citrus like a humid atmosphere around their leaves, so the leaves will benefit from a misting now and then with water from a spray bottle as well as a wipe with a cloth to remove dust and keep them glossy. Little pruning is required other than to remove dead branches or to form a desirable shape.

No. 3 is ideal. The easiest way to grow a grape in a pot is as a standard, with a single central stem and branches bushing out of the top.

When you have planted your vine, tie the main stem to a cane pushed into the centre of the pot. For the first couple of years, allow side branches to grow unpruned. Then, in the third winter, cut off all the side branches except for five or six at the top of the stem. Chop these back to five buds from the main stem. In early summer, cut back any sideshoots developing from these branches to two leaves beyond the young flowers or developing grapes. The bunches of grapes should soon form, hanging from the top of the vine. In winter, cut the side branches back to within two buds of the main stem. Every year repeat the same procedure.

Cape gooseberry

Its smooth, round fruits look like a small orange, but in fact this South American native (*Physalis edulis*) is related to the tomato – and there's certainly a detectable tomato tang behind the sweetness of the fruit. It's a lovely bushy plant with perfectly heart-shaped leaves and pale yellow, chocolate-splodged flowers and it looks particularly beautiful in early autumn when the fruits ripen inside cases that turn brown and papery like little Chinese lanterns.

Either buy Cape gooseberry as plants or sow seeds in small pots inside in mid-spring, transplanting seedlings to a large pot (at least 30cm diameter) or a grow bag in late spring. Place the containers in a sunny, sheltered spot and feed the plants every fortnight with a high-potash feed once fruits begin to form. When the plant reaches about 30cm high, pinch out the growing shoot to encourage fruiting side shoots and tie these in to a trellis or railings. You can eat these fruits raw or make them into delicious jam. Dwarf varieties such as 'Little Lantern' or 'Dwarf Gold' are ideal for pot growing. Frost will kill the plant though you could try overwintering them in a cool, bright room.

Grapes

What could be more decadent than sitting in a deck chair on your balcony on a sunny afternoon, reaching out to pick a bunch of grapes and eating them in a suitably Cleopatra-like manner? There's no reason why you can't grow grapes even several storeys up. Eat them fresh or squish them for a peppy juice as the ultimate start to the day. 'Seyval Blanc', 'Siegerrebe' and 'New York Muscat' are all good choices, even for cool climates, while 'Brandt' has the added benefit of bearing beautiful purple leaves come autumn.

Growing grapes

You're going to need a large pot to grow a grape vine – about 45cm in diameter and depth. Position the container in a sunny, sheltered position and fill it with compost – John Innes

Inspiration
A TROPICAL ROOF PARADISE AMID THE CARGO SHIPS

Victoria Dock in Mumbai, India, is not an area known for its gardens. A busy industrial zone where vast ships load up with cargo and train tracks criss-cross roads thundering with trucks, it's an arid landscape, the skyline full of cranes and faceless office blocks. But there is a hidden gem amongst all this industrial dust: on the roof of the dock workers' staff canteen is a jungle of edible exotica, an oasis of tropical fruit trees, herbs and vegetables – from bananas to pineapples and coconuts.

Created by the canteen's catering officer Preeti Patil (above), this rooftop garden is a testament to recycling and resourcefulness. Vegetables are grown in plastic wastebaskets while fruit trees are happy in scrap oil drums cut in half with the bottoms removed and holes drilled into the sides. A mature banana grows in an 20cm-high bed edged with bricks that has been built straight onto the roof slab.

This 280-square-metre paradise of lemons, chikoo (sapodilla), cashew nuts, mango, pomegranates, custard apple, gourds and guavas is all the more inspiring when you realise that, eight years ago, it was an empty tiled roof, a place only to dump the kitchen rubbish. Now there are 120 varieties of trees, shrubs, climbers and herbs – from lemon grass to ginger, mint and basil, many of which are made into refreshing teas – and butterflies and bees flit among the branches.

Most of us are content with growing in shop-bought multipurpose compost, but Patil believes the secret of her garden's success is a special compost mix made by mixing cow dung, cow urine and black jaggery (or overripe fruit such as bananas) with water and leaving it to ferment before diluting. This mixture is then combined with decomposing plant material and topsoil and left to rot down into a light, fluffy compost with excellent nutrient and water-holding capabilities.

'My produce is safe,' says Patil. 'There's plenty of sunlight, and no rats or cats to disturb anything. The next experiment is to grow rice, and grapes!'

Other exotic edibles

Kiwi fruit

See p. 146.

Chillies

For authentic Mexican food try growing your own Jalapeno chillies, for Thai dishes go for Thai Bird's Eye, and for Italian, you can't go wrong with Etna. See p. 50 for sowing and growing instructions. If you want to keep plants going for more than one year, overwinter them inside.

Lemongrass

This tropical grass with its delicious citronella scent needs a very sunny spot and is frost-tender, so it must be brought into the house in autumn until late spring. With this care, one plant should keep going for several years. Buy plants rather than seeds in spring. When the plant gets too congested, divide it with a sharp knife, and replant it into two separate pots.

It is the rhizomes, the swollen bases of the stems, of this plant that are used in much Asian cooking. In cooler climates, thick stems may be hard to achieve, but you can still use the thin stems – you may just need more of them. For an invigorating tea, steep three or four roughly torn lemongrass leaves in boiling water for five minutes. It also makes a delicious cordial, right.

Peaches and apricots

See p. 112.

Thai basil

This classic Thai ingredient has an aniseedy scent and taste. Purple stems and green leaves make it an unusual addition both to food and to the garden. Sow seeds as for any basil (see p. 45) and bring plants inside before the first frosts.

Pak choi

If you want your outdoor larder to provide you with the ingredients you need to rustle up some exotic Eastern cuisine, you'll need some crunchy pak choi to go with your homegrown chillies and lemongrass. It's fast-growing and will be happy in window boxes as well as in larger containers.

'China Choy' is a good variety – generally the greener-stemmed varieties are tastier. For summer leaves, sow seeds 2cm deep in late spring to early summer; if you want baby leaves to eat raw in salads, thin the seedlings when they emerge to 8cm apart. For mature plants to eat steamed or stir-fried, thin to 15cm apart. Sow again in mid-summer for plants that will last through to the cold winter months.

Melons

Sprawling plants that will soon travel out of their pot and over the floor unless you train them, melons are sweet succulence itself. But those gardening in less than balmy climates should choose varieties carefully. Cantaloupe varieties such as Minnesota Midget or Musketeer are best suited to container growing in cooler climates. Sow and grow as for courgettes or squashes, see p. 49, in containers at least 45cm in depth and diameter. Place in the sunniest, most sheltered spot and harvest when the melons smell delicious.

Project
Lemongrass cordial

WHEN TO DO: ALL YEAR ROUND
You will need:

* 300ml water
* 200g caster sugar
* 3 stalks lemongrass (6 if they're thin)
* 2cm piece fresh ginger, grated
* Grated zest and juice of 1 lemon

Combine the water, caster sugar, lemongrass, ginger and the lemon juice and zest in a pan and heat gently, stirring, until the sugar dissolves. Increase the heat and simmer for 3–4 minutes until thickened. Cool, then strain.

To serve, dilute with sparkling water and serve with a sprig of fresh mint.

The ice and a slice balcony

An allotment on high isn't for everyone, and edible balconies don't have to be all about carrots and beans. Some of us just want to sip a mojito made with our own mint while sitting back and gazing over the city skyline after a hard day's work.

So here's how to grow a delectable balcony banquet of beautiful edible flowers to turn salads into something very special, and juicy fresh fruits to transform cocktails and smoothies.

Inspiration

COCKTAILS ON THE ROOF

Six floors above a busy shopping street in Kensington, west London, sits a beautiful indulgence – a pleasure garden where a stream wends its way through woodlands, olive trees grace a Spanish garden and flamingos strut their stuff. This is the biggest roof garden in Europe and it's been here, astonishingly, since 1938.

Designed by Ralph Hancock, fresh from building the Rockefeller Centre in New York, the pleasure garden originally graced the roof of the chi-chi department store Derry and Toms, and then in the 1970s the building became the premises of Biba, the legendary store that sold everything from clothes to baked beans. The Biba years saw penguins joining the flamingos – until they started stealing food and had to go.

With mature trees growing in only 45cm of soil, it's a magical place, its 2.4m walls giving it a real sense of shelter and peace. You can hardly hear the traffic 30m below. Only the staggering views over London's St Paul's and Royal Albert Hall remind you that you're in the heart of the metropolis.

The top 5 fruits and flowers for the ice and a slice balcony

* Violas
* Borage
* Alpine (woodland or wild) strawberries
* Blueberries
* Nasturtiums

The roof site is now a nightclub, restaurant and bar where people can sashay through the palm trees, figs and olives of the Spanish garden or wander through the Tudor garden's faux-lichened archways. Restraint is not a word you would apply to the Kensington Roof Gardens; they're kitsch, fabulous and all about pleasure.

Head gardener David Lewis has embraced this principle when it comes to the edible plants in the design scheme. Not only do mature figs, olives, peaches and almond trees send you headlong into a Mediterranean fantasy, but the woodland area is full of wild garlic, carrots, blackberries and gooseberries – a forager's paradise. Elsewhere, chillies and courgettes burst out of pots and pumpkins grow in planters on the terrace outside the restaurant, while, a busy collection of edible planters produces hedonistic treats for the bar's cocktail list.

From sumptuous red hibiscus flowers in syrup to the ephemeral glories of day lilies, asters, violas and lavender, edible flowers grace salads in the restaurant or add the final decadent touch to a drink. Courgette flowers are picked, stuffed with ricotta, battered and fried; golden raspberries gleam from the plates and rose petals from the Spanish garden float in cocktails.

Project

A PIMM'S AND MOJITO POT

Two cocktails from one pot – what could be finer? Here's all you need to make two of the summer's most defining and refreshing drinks and to create a colourful container in your garden; the combination of jewel-like alpine strawberries and lush, green mint is offset by the glorious cerulean blue flowers of the borage. Wild strawberries have a much more aromatic, intense flavour than the larger cultivated varieties, but they also add something to the finished cocktail.

WHEN TO DO: EARLY SUMMER

You will need

✳ Crocks, shingle or polystyrene pieces
✳ 1 large pot about 40cm in diameter
✳ Multipurpose compost
✳ 1 × 20cm diameter plastic pot with the bottom cut off
✳ 1 mint plant – spearmint (or garden mint) is best, but any is fine
✳ 2 wild strawberry plants (also known as alpine or woodland strawberry), such as 'Mignonette' or 'Alexandria'
✳ 1 borage plant

How to do it

Add a layer of crocks, shingle or chunks of broken polystyrene to the bottom of the large pot, then fill it two-thirds full with compost. Make a hollow with your hands at one side of the pot and push the bottomless 20cm pot in so that that rim is just above the level of the compost.

Plant the mint in this smaller pot, adding more compost to firm it in well. This confines the roots of the mint, otherwise it would take over the container. Then plant the strawberries and the borage in the remaining space, making sure the strawberries are near the edge. Water well and place in a sunny, sheltered spot.

Inspired to have a sky-high pleasure zone? Why not plant up some deliciously decadent pots of your own?

MOJITO
Makes 1 glass

※ 14 freshly picked mint
  leaves, plus a sprig
  to decorate
※ 1½ teaspoons white
  caster sugar
※ juice of ½ lime
※ 4 large ice cubes
※ 2 measures light rum
※ 2 splashes Angostura
  bitters
※ sparkling mineral water

Put the mint, sugar and lime
juice in a glass tumbler and
bash everything together
with the back of a fork. Crush
the ice cubes in a pestle and
mortar and spoon into the
glass. Add the rum and
Angostura bitters, then top
with sparkling water and
decorate with a sprig of mint.

PIMM'S
Serves 6

※ 1 bottle of Pimm's
  No.1 Cup
※ 1 large bottle lemonade
※ plenty of ice cubes
※ 2 handfuls freshly
  picked wild strawberries
※ 1 handful freshly
  picked mint sprigs
※ 10 borage flowers

Mix the Pimm's with the
lemonade in a large jug
according to the instructions
on the bottle, leaving a third
at the top to allow for the
fruit and ice. Add the ice
cubes, strawberries and
mint. Stir, then scatter over
the borage flowers just
before serving.

Project
EDIBLE FLOWER POT FOR DECADENT SALADS

This container makes for a riot of colour – and you can eat the flowers too. The silky nasturtium blooms are produced from early summer right through to late autumn in an orgy of yellows, oranges and retina-burning reds. Viola flowers have purple petals and blushing yellow throats and are produced in profusion from mid-summer right through to late autumn, if regularly deadheaded. Sow seeds for both inside in mid-spring and transplant outside when they're about 3cm tall, or pick up a tray of plug plants from a garden centre. If you have any plants left over after planting up this pot, push them into hanging baskets or in among salad leaves in containers.

Day lilies are decadence itself: large, waxy flowers of all hues, they're almost artificial in their perfection. True to their name, the flowers do last for only a day, but they are produced in profusion throughout the summer, so you always seem to have more: a real showstopper. In autumn, when the leaves turn brown, cut them back; the plants are perennial, so they will come back each spring, although they may need to be divided after a few years to stop them becoming congested, which can prevent them flowering.

WHEN TO DO:
MID-SPRING TO EARLY SUMMER
You will need
* ❋ Crocks or polystyrene pieces
* ❋ 1 large pot about 40cm in diameter
* ❋ Multipurpose compost
* ❋ 1 day lily (hemerocallis) plant, ideally a dwarf variety such as 'Stella d'Oro'
* ❋ 6 *Viola tricolor* (heartsease) or *Viola odorata*, either bought as plug plants or grown from seed sown inside in small pots in mid-spring
* ❋ 3 nasturtiums – either buy as plants or sow direct into the pot about 3cm deep from mid-spring to mid-summer. A compact variety such as 'Empress of India' with deep, velvety reds and oranges is ideal

How to do it:
Add a layer of crocks or polystyrene chunks to the bottom of the pot, then fill almost to the top with compost. Plant the day lily in the centre, encircled by the violas, then plant the nasturtiums around the edge so they can trail down over the sides of the pot. Water well.

After a month or so, the exquisite flowers can be picked and strewn onto the tops of salads. The violas and nasturtiums (remove the stamens before eating) can be eaten whole and have a refreshing peppery taste. You can also eat the nasturtium leaves – chopped and added to mashed potato they give it a crunchy, peppery kick – and, at the end of the season, the seed pods, which you can eat fresh or pickle like capers. Day lilies taste a bit like sweet lettuce – pull the petals off and scatter them individually over salads.

Other ideas for cocktails, drinks and salads

Golden raspberries such as 'All Gold' can be grown in a pot about 45cm in diameter. A handful of the fruits in a glass of sparkling wine is a bit different. Grow these as for regular raspberries, see p. 99.

Cape gooseberry or *Physalis edulis* can be grown in a pot and will produce intriguing, papery-cased, golden fruits with a tangy, sweet taste. Just one added as a finishing touch to a dessert or in a drink makes a real impact.

Blueberries are easy to grow in pots and are productive from mid-summer right up to late autumn. They are great for adding to drinks whole or crushed in smoothies. See p. 51 for growing instructions.

Pot marigolds (*Calendula officinalis*) produce vivid orange blooms that look lovely scattered on the top of salads. Sow seeds in seed trays inside from early spring, or direct into the pot in late spring, or buy plug plants.

Chives, left to bloom, produce purple pom-pom flowers that look great in salads.

Chamomile (*Chamaemelum nobile*) or Roman chamomile has pineapple-scented, daisy-like flowers that make delicious, soothing tea. An annual, chamomile seeds should be sown in mid-spring direct into window boxes, hanging baskets or medium-sized containers, or buy plants in late spring/early summer.

Runner bean flowers, with their vivid colour and delicate beany taste, are delightful in salads – and if you're growing plants for their pods anyway, they are no trouble to get hold of.

Courgette flowers are delicious stuffed with cream cheese and pine nuts then dipped in batter and fried until golden. Use the male flowers – the ones at the end of a narrow stalk – as opposed to the female ones that show a baby courgette swelling behind them.

The
Edible
Forest
Roof
Garden

This is one for the serious rooftop gardener; it's about as far away as possible from bunging a few window boxes outside. Urban food farming doesn't get much more ambitious than creating an edible forest on a roof; you'll need the input of a landscaper, not to mention a structural engineer, but what rewards! And what inspiration, even for the small-scale balcony gardener – you can be sitting in the middle of a town but lost in a woodland wonderland, idly wandering the paths and picking cherries. It's incredible that 3m trees can be happy growing in just 30cm of soil, but prepare it right and you can create a fully grown edible forest.

Inspiration
STAIRWAY TO A HAVEN

Nowhere is this urban farming model more inspirational than at the Reading International Solidarity Centre garden in the south of England. There, the rooftop oasis leads you on a world tour of bizarre and beautiful edibles; from Chilean guava to medlars, Japanese wineberries, shitake mushrooms and crunchy oca tubers. There are mature cherries, cobnuts, pears and apples, but other less obvious edible trees, too, all with food or medicinal uses. Willy Wonka-style blue beanpods hang from the blue sausage fruit tree (*Decaisnea fargesii*), clusters of weird pink spiky balls adorn the strawberry tree, and the toothache tree (*Zanthoxylum alatum planispinum*) is sprinkled with vivid red, peppercorn-like berries that, when chewed, fill your mouth with spices. Elsewhere a Juneberry tree, dotted with tiny, sweet, red berries, nestles next to the broad, exotically glossy canopy of a loquat.

The fences and walls of this garden are thick with vines – grapes, kiwis, hops – and canes of wineberries and raspberries. Along the sides of the woodland-style paths, mulched with woodchips and shingle, grow wild garlic, wasabi, Solomon's seal, sorrel and wild strawberries from the regular woodland variety to the bizarre hairy fruits of the Plymouth strawberry. In autumn, a fat windfall medlar fruit lies on the forest floor, its flesh pulpy and sweet. Everywhere you look a plant reveals itself to be intriguing and extraordinary – if not always at first sight, then at first taste – such as with stevia, the super-sweet leaf once commonly used as a sugar, or the exquisite wild-strawberry-flavoured berries of the Chilean guava bush.

Solar panels and a wind turbine power a pump for a rainwater storage system, materials are recycled, waste food from the café downstairs is composted, and animal life is encouraged with strategically placed nesting boxes and piles of logs. A thick layer of mulch retains moisture in the soil and keeps down weeds, while sprawling strawberries and herbs do the same job.

This is not just a roof garden, it's a roof forest: a living, breathing, self-sustaining ecosystem that mimics the multiple layers of vegetation found in the wild – fruit and nut trees are underplanted with berry fruits that are happy in their dappled shade, and beneath them are herbs and low-lying vegetables and fruit. Unlike traditional fruit and vegetable gardens, where many crops are replaced each year with new seedlings, these edible forest plants will live for several years, producing fruit, leaves and nuts. This is a low-maintenance, more natural model of food production – permaculture in the sky.

STEAL THEIR STYLE: CREATE A MINI EDIBLE FOREST

An edible roof garden such as this one is surprisingly low-maintenance since most of the crops are perennial. Berries, vines and fruit trees once planted will last for years, requiring only a little pruning and giving lots of fruit in return. Herbs such as thyme and mint are similarly long-lived, as are strawberries and sorrel. All grow easily in pots and require less effort than annual crops – none of that fiddling with seedlings every spring.

Try to be sustainable, storing rainwater whenever you can – in water butts or even buckets. Consider keeping a wormery to turn your kitchen scraps into compost. Mulch containers with anything that will help keep moisture in the soil. When planting, try to combine crops so that they can benefit from each other, underplanting climbers and shrubs with groundcovering perennials that can shade and retain moisture in their roots – a hardy kiwi, for example, underplanted with wild strawberries.

Project
MAKE A LOW-TECH WATERING SYSTEM

You don't need an automatic watering system to keep your plants happy. A collection of containers or a raised bed will really benefit from the gradual drip-drip from seep hose fed by a bucket raised on bricks. All of the items needed items are available in garden or DIY stores.

You will need
* A household drill
* 1 sturdy bucket
* A plastic tap (such as those for water butts)
* 4 or 5 bricks (or similar) to stand the bucket on
* A length of seep or soaker hosing, perforated or garden hose with holes made in the side
* 1 plug or stopper for the end of the hose

How to do it
Drill a hole in the side of the bucket near the bottom and push the tap into it so that it fits snugly. Stand it on the bricks, then attach the hose to the tap and lay the hose on the soil surface, weaving it around your plants. Put the plug in the open end of the hose. Fill the bucket with water. Slowly, the water will seep out of the holes in the hose into the soil around the plants roots just where they need it, making your watering less frequent and less fiddly. The bucket will catch rainwater too.

Classic edible-forest roof crops, working from the canopy down

Tall crops: Apples, pears, plums, cherries, quinces, olives, peaches, apricots, figs, strawberry trees (*Arbutus andrachne*), loquats, cobnuts, mulberries, Juneberries

Scrambling vines and sprawling canes: Grapes, hardy kiwis (*Actinidia arguta* 'Issai'), raspberries, Japanese wineberries (*Rubus phoenicolasius*), edible passionflowers (Passiflora edulis), loganberries, blackberries, tayberries, boysenberries

Shrubs: Blueberries, Chilean guavas, Goji berries, gooseberries, cranberries, jostaberry

Medium plants: Lemon verbena, rosemary, sage, lavender, valerian, mint, sorrel

Ground cover: Wild (woodland) strawberry, oca (*Oxalis tuberosa*), sorrel, garlic chives, chives, wild garlic, lemon balm, thyme, oregano, wasabi, Plymouth strawberries

The top 5 unusual crops for an edible forest roof

Kiwi fruit

These are vines, so they will romp up supports and make quite impressive plants with a really jungly feel. In cooler climates, choose a hardy kiwi (*Actinidia arguta*), such as 'Issai', which produces bunches of deliciously sweet, grape-sized fruit that you eat with the skins on (they're not hairy like regular kiwis). They can survive extremely cold winters and, if pruned properly, produce a good crop. For regular-sized fruits try *Actinidia deliciosa*, particularly the variety 'Jenny', which is self-fertile so you'll need only the one plant.

Plant kiwi fruits in a large pot at least 30cm in diameter filled with multipurpose compost or John Innes No. 3 and place in a sheltered, sunny position, protecting young shoots from frost in early spring. Without pruning, the vine will clamber all over the place and produce few fruits, so it's well worth keeping it in check.

Fix parallel wires to a wall about 45cm apart or provide a trellis for the vine to climb up. Push a long bamboo cane into the pot and tie it to the wall supports. When the vine reaches the bottom support wire, rub out all but three shoots, tying the uppermost one to the cane and the others to the horizontal wire on each side of the main stem. These sideshoots are now called 'laterals'.

When the vine reaches the second wire (or grows about another 45cm, if using a trellis), tie in two further side shoots to the wire, rubbing out any other new ones, to form two further laterals. Prune the laterals when they are about 90cm long to encourage sideshoots to form along their length. As the plant continues to grow, pinch these sideshoots back to five leaves – it's from these sideshoots that fruiting spurs will develop. In the winter, prune back the sideshoots to two buds beyond where the fruit was borne the previous summer.

Alternatively, if you want a more jungly look to your vine, and fruit production is less of a priority, cut out flowered stems in spring to allow the new stems space to grow and develop.

Japanese wineberry

Even in winter, this relative of the raspberry, *Rubus phoenicolasius*, makes a stunning sight and a real talking point, with its brilliant pink stems covered in orange hairy spines. In winter sunlight the spines are breathtaking. Its small orange-red berries are succulent and sweeter than raspberries.

Grow it as you would a raspberry, planting it in a large pot at least 45cm in diameter and cutting down fruited canes to the ground in late summer, then tying in strong new canes to wires attached to the wall. If you tie the stems into a fan shape the plant looks pretty all year round. Alternatively, grow it in a freestanding pot – the stems will droop artistically.

Goji berry

A 'superfood' with 500 times the amount of vitamin C by weight as oranges, goji plants (*Lycium barbarum*) are shrubby bushes with bright red, rosehip-like berries. Native to the Himalayas, they are known there as 'happy berries' because of the feeling of wellbeing they are said to induce when eaten.

Plant in full sun in a large container at least 30cm in diameter. The plants grow fast, reaching up to 1.2m tall in a pot, and can produce a kilogram of fruit in their second year. Wind- and drought-tolerant, they are easygoing plants and excellent for a rooftop. Eat the berries fresh and enjoy the liquorice taste, or try them dried, when they taste a little like cranberries – you can dry them yourself and add them to muesli for a power-packed start to the day.

Oca

This unusual tuber (*Oxalis tuberosa*) from South America looks a bit like a small potato or a Chinese artichoke. You can boil or roast oca, but it is best eaten raw, when it has a lovely fresh crunch and a lemony taste. Plant it from late spring when fear of frost has passed in containers about 20cm apart . The leaves will sprawl everywhere, though you can tie them into an upright support to keep them tidy.

The most unusual thing about oca is that you don't harvest the crop until late autumn, even early winter, after the frosts. Even if the foliage is frosted and dead, the tubers will still keep growing underground. Leave a few tubers in the pot when you harvest them and you will have more next year.

Chilean guava

See p. 59.

A kiwi vine in full blossom, left, and the vivid pink stems of a Japanese wineberry, right

The Futuristic Balcony

Imagine plucking your own beans, strawberries and tomatoes from the wall outside your kitchen door from a vertical garden that could fit into the tiniest balcony space but that would provide fresh crops all year round. And without any input from you. All you would have to do is plant up your modular wall, turn on the automatic watering and feeding system, then stand back and watch the plants grow. No soil, no watering, just fresh food every day of the year. Now imagine whole city apartment blocks clothed with these sleek mounted panels, all providing fresh food right in the heart of cities from Dubai to New York. No longer grey and sterile, city skyscapes would be filled with towers of tumbling, green, modern-day Hanging Gardens of Babylon. This scenario may not yet be a reality, but one thing is for sure, the future of food production is looking up.

Vertical farming

If climate change and population growth continue at their present levels, scientists claim that farming as we know it will no longer exist within 50 years. Fifty per cent of the world is now urbanised – by 2050 that figure will have risen to 80 per cent. And as the global population grows, available agricultural land is shrinking. In 1970 there was roughly one acre of farmland available for each person in the world, but by 2000 it had reduced to half an acre. By 2050 the United Nations predicts that it will drop to a third of an acre per person. How, quite simply, are we going to feed everybody?

For some, the answer could be vertical farms – vast steel towers in the heart of cities growing fruit and vegetable crops hydroponically (that is, using chemical nutrients rather than traditional soil). Rather than having to transport crops into the cities, which uses up valuable fuel and resources, why not grow them right there in the metropolis? A 30-storey building covering a full city block (about five acres), could feed 50,000 people a year, according to the author of *The Vertical Farm*, Dickson Despommier, a professor at Columbia University. This is the world of agritecture: buildings designed to produce food on a mass scale. Images of how these towers might look are seductive – the transparent walls needed to let light in for growing crops making them look like futuristic Hanging Gardens of Babylon – yet up to this point the costs of building them have been prohibitive.

Perhaps more realistic are the urban food-growing ideas of aerospace engineer and New York University professor Natalie Jeremijenko, whose bug-like pods are designed to perch on the roofs of skyscrapers. With their splayed stilt legs that would spread weight onto the loadbearing walls and a streamlined shape that would not only maximise sun exposure but minimise wind resistance, these greenhouses could sit on any unoccupied city rooftop, packed with crops growing in soil-free hydroponic trays.

Say goodbye to soil?

Hydroponics is the cultivation of plants in a nutrient solution rather than in soil. Plants are rooted into a lightweight, inert medium such as rockwool, and then fed and watered with a nutrient solution. Productivity is greatly increased when crops are grown this way (from double to ten times the quantity of crops produced) and waste materials can be recycled. Hydroponic cultivation uses at least 20 per cent less water than conventional growing, and there are no soil-borne pests and diseases to contend with, either.

Hydroponics are already transforming city rooftops. In 2010, Gotham Greens began planting rooftop farms in Queens and Brooklyn, in New York, growing salad and herbs hydroponically in greenhouses using renewable energy and captured rainwater. They will sell their produce to the natural and organic food store Whole Foods, who have branches across the city. The educational organisation New York Sun Works projects that hydroponic farms spread over New York's 14,000 acres of unshaded rooftop could feed as many as 20 million people a year.

But how do these futuristic projections affect the domestic balcony or rooftop gardener? Put simply, there may come a time in the not too distant future when city apartment blocks might be covered in crops, growing out from the sides of the building and feeding the inhabitants within. On a more domestic scale, each apartment could come with its own edible wall on the balcony or even inside the building.

A potential glimpse into the future can be found in Shoreditch, east London, where a 2 × 4m wall brims with salad and herbs (see p. 151), providing customers of the Waterhouse Restaurant with both a wonderfully modern and vibrant backdrop and a delicious lunch. Supplied by Biotecture UK, a leading designer of green walls, the wall combines frilly lettuces, spinach, rocket and parsley that grow tantalisingly within reach, and soon cover the modular framework in a beautiful map of purples and greens. The edible walls are made

up of modules filled with rockwool, through which plug plants are pushed and into which they root. They are then fed and watered hydroponically.

The possibilities for such a system for domestic roofs and balconies are enormous, and Biotecture UK is now working on a small-scale, cost-effective model. The company's designer, Mark Laurence, believes this technology would be particularly effective in the developing world. As it is more energy-efficient than traditional growing, the potential for such a technology to feed people in cities is enormous.

Laurence is currently adapting the company's Biowall so that it can grow vegetable and fruit plants such as courgettes, French beans and tomatoes, working on its sustainability by making it easier to recycle the growing medium. He envisions a time not so far ahead when people living in cities could have their own personal edible wall on their balcony. They could receive pre-grown seedlings in the post to plant up and would then need to fill a water tank every so often that would trickle water and nutrients down to the plants' roots. Once the vegetables had been harvested, the rockwool blocks they grew in could be taken to an urban recycling centre to be replaced by fresh ones. It's a simple solution, one with no electricity required, no daily watering hassle and no heavy compost to lug up several storeys.

And to those critics of hydroponics who say it is environmentally unsound because the feeds are non-organic, Mark says: 'There's no reason why you couldn't use wormery feed, comfrey or seaweed.'

The Urb Garden, designed by Xavier Callaud, incorporates just such an idea. In this cabinet-sized edible wall, the perfect size for a small domestic balcony, strawberries, tomatoes, salad and herbs grow in traditional garden compost rather than hydroponic material, but they are fed by an integral wormery into which you add your kitchen scraps. A foot pump takes the feed and water up to the top of the wall

where it drips down, and after each crop compost can be replaced using fertile worm casts – a beautifully sustainable system.

Callaud's idea is currently a prototype, but it's only a question of time before this product, and others like it, take the urban growing-your-own revolution that exciting step further. The next few decades will be crunch time for urban food production. There's no doubt that cities will have to adapt to produce crops to help feed the world's growing population, but whether they'll be doing it in bug-shaped pods on the roof, up the sides of vast skyscrapers or in domestic-scale panels outside every apartment owner's kitchen window, only time will tell. One thing is for certain, the urban landscape will look very different in 50 years time – who knows, it might even be a little bit greener.

Hydroponic crops – the future of urban food production?

Pests and Diseases

Aphids

See Blackfly, Greenfly and Woolly aphid.

Apple and pear scab

Rain and wind spread the spores of this fungal disease that causes dark green patches to appear on the leaves of apple and pear trees and then corky scabs on the surface of the fruit. Remove and throw away fallen leaves to reduce the spread of the spores.

Apple sawfly

Adult sawflies lay their eggs in apple blossom. When they hatch the larvae create scar-like markings on the fruit which then fail to develop, dropping off in early summer. Remove any damaged fruit you see on the tree or on the ground – and throw it away rather than composting them.

Bacterial canker

This disease affects stone fruit trees, such as peaches, plums, cherries and apricots, causing a clear brown gum to ooze from the branches. Prune out affected areas down to at least 20cm below the canker and throw prunings away rather than composting them. To deter, prune stone fruits only in the summer months.

Birds

The fruit of trees such as plums, cherries and peaches is a magnet for many birds, while brassicas can be targeted by pigeons. If you're really bothered, you may have to net the trees or plants at vulnerable times. With trees, you could also try hanging plastic bottles, Dvds or glass candleholders in the branches to deter the birds.

Blackfly

These little black aphids can be a particular problem on beans, clustering around the growing tips and sucking the sap. Either blast off the flies with a jet of the hose or brush them off or spray them with insecticidal soft soap – an organic aphid deterrent available from all garden centres. (You'll need a plastic bottle with a nozzle to spray it on with.) Alternatively, a few drops of washing-up liquid diluted in water and sprayed on also sees them off.

Blight

This is an airborne fungal disease that tends to strike in damp, cool summers, affecting tomatoes and potatoes. It is unlikely to be a problem for potatoes on balconies, since container-grown spuds are usually First or Second Earlies, ready for harvest before the disease takes hold. Look

Netting can protect
brassicas from
piegeons and butterflies
whose eggs hatch
into leaf-munching
caterpillars

Blossom wilt

If new shoots on your fruit tree
suddenly wilt, particularly if it's a few
weeks after flowering, chances are
your tree is suffering from this fungal
disease. Apples, pears, plums, cherries,
nectarines, peaches and apricots can
be affected. Avoid by removing any
mummified fruit – throwing it away
rather than composting it – and
pruning out any diseased spurs
over winter.

Botrytis

The tell-tale sign is a grey, furry mould
on leaves or fruits. Remove any infected
material and take care when planting
lettuces not to bury the bottom leaves
in the compost.

Brown scale insect

This is a pest of citrus and bay trees.
Shield-like bugs cluster in the leaf
joints and under leaves, sucking the sap
and weakening the plant. Remove the
insects by hand or with an old
toothbrush and soapy water.

Carrot fly

This is generally not a problem for
balcony or rooftop gardeners since
these pests can't fly higher than
60cm.

Caterpillars

Large holes in leaves without any
slug or snail trails generally suggests
caterpillars have been visiting.
Look under the leaves for the culprits
as well as for clusters of caterpillar
eggs and squash them.

for brown patches on leaves with white
rings on the underside and, if you see
them, dig up potatoes immediately.
Tomato stems may also show brown
patches and their fruits can turn black
and rotten overnight. With tomatoes,
cutting off affected leaves and fruit as
soon as you spot blight may stop the
disease from spreading through the
plant. If blight has struck your tomatoes
or potatoes, don't compost the leaves
since the spores can survive in the bin,
affecting future crops. Instead, throw
them away.

Blossom end rot

A dark, leathery patch on the bottom of
tomatoes indicates this problem, which
is caused by irregular watering. Cut off
affected fruits and prevent the issue
arising by watering little and often
rather than via an occasional deluge.

Cats

Cats can be a real pain, scratching up the compost of newly sown containers and using them as toilets. Twiggy or prickly sticks laid across or poked upright into the compost will generally put them off.

Codling moth

Watch out for this pest on apple and pear trees – the larvae tunnel into the fruit, not only spoiling it but also encouraging secondary rots to form. Deter by putting up codling moth traps in late spring.

Common scab

Scabby, scurfy patches on the skin of potatoes are superficial and won't affect their flavour. Simply scrub off the marks before cooking.

Flea beetle

Tiny holes in rocket and brassicas and a cloud of tiny black beetles that fly up when disturbed usually means flea beetle. A mild infestation doesn't do too much harm, but if it's a real problem, avoid growing rocket between late May and mid-summer when flea beetle are most prolific.

Greenfly

These are aphids that suck the sap from the growing tips of many vegetable and fruit plants, whose excretions encourage fungal diseases. Spray any bugs you see with insecticidal soft-soap solution or a few drops of washing-up liquid diluted with water in a spray bottle.

Leaf miner

Chard, spinach and beetroot leaves can be bothered by this pest, tiny larvae which make tunnels inside the leaves, causing dead, brown patches. Either remove individual leaves or squish the larvae inside the leaf with your fingers.

Peach leaf curl

This is a fungal disease affecting peach, nectarine and apricot trees which causes the leaves to turn red and pucker before falling off. The spores are spread by rain splash, so contain the disease by covering fan-trained trees with a sheet of plastic from autumn to mid-spring (allowing air to get into the sides). Do the same with standard potted trees or bring them inside over the winter until mid-spring. It's also worth investigating growing disease-resistant varieties.

Powdery mildew

Peas, apples, grapes, melons, courgettes, squashes, pumpkins and cucumbers are susceptible to this fungal disease, which makes it look as though the leaves are sprinkled with talcum powder. Improve air flow around the plants by removing leaves or even entire plants, feed regularly and don't let the compost dry out.

Raspberry beetle

These beetles lay their eggs inside blackberries and raspberries, making them brown, hard and inedible. Little white grubs may be found inside berries, so soak the fruits in salty water to bring the creatures out, then rinse thoroughly before eating.

Red spider mite

This is usually a greenhouse pest, but occasionally it can be a problem in dry, hot summers for citrus, cucumber and pepper plants. Microscopic insects colonise the leaves, sucking the sap and weakening the plant. The signs to look out for are pale yellow dots on the undersides of leaves and white web fibres underneath. Mist the leaves to increase humidity. Indoors, the biological control *Phytoseiulus persimilis* can be effective; it is available by mail-order through garden centres or online.

Sciarid fly

Brown flies, about 4mm long, that are found on the surface of moist potting compost, these can be a problem with seedlings, particularly those sown inside in pots in the spring. Their larvae feed on roots, making the plants collapse and die. They thrive in damp conditions so prevent by watering from below and keep watering to a minimum. A layer of grit or sand on the surface of the compost can also help.

Silverleaf

A fungal disease affecting apples and stone fruits such as peaches, plums, apricots and cherries that causes the leaves to become silvery and the tree's growth to be weakened. Avoid by pruning stone fruits only in the summer months. If mildly affected, a tree can be coaxed back to health via plenty of feeding; if severely affected, trees should be removed.

adult beetles, squash them. If you find small, white, U-shaped grubs in the compost and the plant is not too badly affected, shake the compost off the roots, wash them thoroughly and then replant in fresh compost. Throw away the infested compost as it will be full of eggs that you don't want spread around your garden.

Whitefly

Clouds of tiny, white moths that fly up when disturbed suggest a whitefly infestation. Spray an infected plant with insecticidal soft soap or a few drops of washing-up liquid diluted with water in a spray bottle.

Woolly aphid

Apples can be susceptible to these pests that secrete a white, cotton-wool like fluff on the stems in spring and summer. Brush them off with soapy water.

Woolly vine scale

Grapes and currants are particularly susceptible to these flat, brown insects which lay their eggs in cotton-wool-like threads on the bark. Remove with an old toothbrush and soapy water.

Slugs and snails

Slugs and snails can reach the balcony, carried up on pots or in old compost and, once established, can be a real pest even several storeys up. So, discard any snails in household rubbish and keep an eye out for hiding places under pots. Organic slug pellets based on ferric phosphate are harmless to other wildlife and children and are very effective in dealing with slugs.

Split tomatoes

Irregular watering causes the tomatoes to burst, so try to water little and often rather than via an occasional deluge.

Vine weevils

These greyish-black beetles cut slits in the leaves of plants, but it's the grubs that are the real menace for container gardeners, since these eat the roots of plants, killing them. If you find the

Recommended suppliers

Pots, tools and other equipment

The Balcony Gardener
Thebalconygardener.com
Pots, mini raised beds, furniture... stylish stuff chosen with balconies in mind

Earthbox
earthbox.co.uk
These low-maintenance, high-yielding 'self-watering' containers are ideal for roofs and balconies

Faulks & Company
faulks.co.uk
Great for rubber tub trugs – inexpensive planters in all bright colours and sizes

Harrod Horticultural
Harrodhorticultural.com
The Organic Gardening Catalogue
Organiccatalogue.com
Great for basic equipment from raised beds to wigwam supports and tools

Polanter
polanter.co.uk
Wall-mounted planters that make a quirky alternative to hanging baskets

Wiggly Wigglers
Wigglywigglers.co.uk
The place for wormeries – their little Worm Café is ideal for a balcony or roof

Woolly Pockets
gardenbeet.com
Ingenious wall planters made from recycled bottles, great for small spaces

Seeds and Plants

Delfland
Organicplants.co.uk
Quality vegetable plug plants by post

DT Brown
Dtbrownseeds.co.uk
Wide range of vegetable seeds and plants

Jekka's Herb Farm
Jekkasherbfarm.com
The place to go for every herb you'll ever need – and some you've never even heard of

Ken Muir
Kenmuir.co.uk
Great fruit specialist supplying a range from apple trees to kiwi fruit

Pennard Plants
Pennardplants.com
Wide selection of fruit and veg seeds, from the ordinary to the unusual – wonderberry anyone?

Rocket Gardens
Rocketgardens.co.uk
Instant well-priced vegetable gardens – pop the seedlings in a pot and you're away

Sarah Raven
Sarahraven.com
Seeds and seedlings plus gorgeous gardening accessories – particularly interesting range of salad leaves and edible flowers

Seeds of Italy
Generous-sized packets of salad and vegetable seeds with an Italian flavour – beans, squashes and salads a speciality

Suttons
Suttons.co.uk
Good for seeds and plants, particularly for container crops

Thompson and Morgan
Thompson-morgan.com
Large seed range, great selection of seed potatoes

Other resources

City Farmer
Cityfarmer.info
Vancouver-based website that not only gives some great tips on growing food on roofs and balconies but also collates urban farming news from all over the world

Eagle Street Rooftop Farm
rooftopfarms.org
Growing inspiration from a 6,000-square-foot vegetable farm on the top of an old bagel factory in Brooklyn, New York, complete with chickens

Freecycle
Uk.freecyle.org
Find your nearest group online and look out for salvaged and recycled pieces to give your balcony that personal touch. Best of all, it's free

growingCities
growingcities.blogspot.com
Vibrant online hub for the urban farming movement based in the US but collating stories from all over the world

Reading International Solidarity Centre Edible Forest Rooftop Garden
risc.org.uk/gardens
Stacks of information here about how this astonishing English roof garden was constructed, including useful plant lists and links to other urban rooftop gardens worldwide

Société Centrale d'Apiculture
la-sca.net
The society for French beekeepers. Budding Parisian beekeepers can enrol on courses in the Jardins du Luxembourg

Templeman Harrison
A garden design business that creates inspirational, unique landscapes.
www.templemanharrison.com

Urban Beekeeping
Urbanbeekeeping.co.uk
Newbie London urban beekeepers can find advice and courses here. Look online for the beekeeping association nearest to you

The Vertical Farm – Feeding the World in the 21st Century by Dr Dickson Despommier (St Martin's Press) Growing crops in cities down the sides of tower blocks – is this the future of global food production? Dr Despommier certainly thinks so

Vertical Veg
Verticalveg.org.uk
Tips and inspiration from London balcony grower Mark Ridsdill Smith on how to produce the most food possible in a small space

Uncommon Ground, Chicago, the first organic rooftop farm in the USA
eatthisgrowthat.blogspot.com
Chicago restaurant Uncommon Ground grows much of its own food on the roof – this useful blog shows how they manage it

Urban Leaves
urbanleavesinindia.com
Follow the progress of Preeti Patil's stunning terrace garden in Mumbai.

Great tips on making compost and growing in containers

Urban Organic Gardener
urbanorganicgardener.com
Mike Lieberman has gone from a tiny fire escape in Manhattan to a balcony in Los Angeles, growing as much food as he can along the way – follow his resourceful edible growing projects here

Index

Acknowledgements

I couldn't have written this book without the help of the following people. Big thanks to:

Heather and Elly, Judith and Vicki at Kyle Cathie, Sarah for taking the gorgeous photos, not to mention her help with the heavy lifting, and to Ali the stylist.

❋ Eagle Street Rooftop Farm's Annie Novak for answering all my questions about city rooftop farming, and for running such an inspirational outfit – why can't we all farm on the roof of former bagel factories in Brooklyn?

❋ The Shoreditch Trust's Chris Reilly, thanks for being so 'can do'

❋ The London Beekeepers' Association's Dr Luke Dixon (urbanbeekeeping.co.uk) for answering all my bee questions so patiently and Nikki Vane for letting us shoot her extraordinary roof garden in London complete with buzzing hives (lbka.org.uk)

❋ Garden designer Charlotte Wess for not only inspiring me to plant things in bike tyres but also for ferrying her fab planters across London in a taxi so I could borrow them

❋ Manhattan fire-escape gardener Mike Lieberman for showing me that small can be beautiful, and that painting plastic milk bottles can look cute

❋ Mark Ridsdill Smith of Vertical Veg for his inspiring recycled balcony, his advice on making self-watering containers and for telling me you can eat sunflower shoots – I'll never look back

❋ Garth Hewitt for letting us take over his Barbican balcony for a morning (sorry about the cherry tomatoes we might have left in the lift)

❋ Liz Fay for letting us shoot her fire escape with a view

❋ Marie Viljoen for letting us use the gorgeous picture of her Manhattan balcony

❋ David Lewis, head gardener at Kensington Roof Gardens, who knows that roof gardens are all about having fun

❋ Helen Cameron of Chicago's Uncommon Ground restaurant for answering my questions and showing me the way to Earthboxes

❋ Dave Richards of the Reading International Solidarity Centre for showing us round his astonishing roof garden, and introducing me to Chilean guava – thanks for the cutting

❋ Mark Laurence of Biotecture for answering all my questions about the future of urban food production and edible walls

❋ Ben Mason for showing us his gorgeous sun-trap roof terrace on a very hot day – thanks for the chilled water and lemon

❋ Anthony Roberts and Michael Waring for letting us shoot their lovely balcony, for being flexible when the sun was too bright and then when it rained, and for looking after my Calamondin orange when the taxi didn't turn up

❋ Jo Behari for her on-the-level DIY advice on flooring and weight restrictions

❋ Wolff Olins' Stuart Robinson for letting us photograph the windy but wonderful roof garden

❋ The Mumbai Port Trust's Preeti Patil for sharing her wisdom about making compost and growing exotic fruit

❋ Paul Richens from Global Generation for showing me some of his fabulous edible roof gardens and answering more questions about wormeries than any one person should ever have to

Additional photography, picture library credits:
❋ p. 5 Clive Nichols ❋ p. 6–7 Marie Viljoen ❋ Derek St Romaine Garden Photo Library p. 37 Peter Cassidy ❋ p. 40 garden picture library/Andrea Jones ❋ p. 45 Peter Cassidy ❋ p. 48 Peter Cassidy ❋ p. 51 GAP/FhF Greenmedia ❋ p. 55 Derek St Romaine Garden Photo Library ❋ p. 79 Clive Nichols ❋ p. 80 Patrick Kovarik/AFP/Getty Images ❋ p. 81 photolibrary/John Carey ❋ p. 83 Adam Golfer ❋ p. 87 Peter Cassidy ❋ p. 96 Clive Nichols ❋ p. 105 Clive Nichols/Designer: Charlotte Rowe, London ❋ p. 112 GAP/Paul Debois ❋ p. 113 GAP/Friedrich Strauss ❋ p. 117 AFP/Getty Images ❋ p. 117 Peter Cassidy ❋ p. 117 Cristian Barnett ❋ p. 125 GAP/Lee Avison ❋ p. 126 Peter Cassidy ❋ p. 143 GAP/Anne Green-Armytage ❋ p. 144 David McLain/Aurora Photos/Corbis ❋ p. 149 GAP/FhF Greenmedia ❋ p. 150 GAP/Lee Avison ❋ p. 152 photolibrary/Photos Lamontagne ❋ p. 153 photolibrary/Mark Bolton

For
Theo and
Arthur